P9-DVC-566

THELONIOUS MONK

His Life and Music

THOMAS FITTERLING

TRANSLATED BY ROBERT DOBBIN
FOREWORD BY STEVE LACY

BERKELEY HILLS BOOKS
Berkeley, California

Published by
Berkeley Hills Books
P.O. Box 9877, Berkeley, California 94709

Copyright © 1997 OREOS VERLAG, Waakirchen (Germany)
This translation © 1997 Berkeley Hills Books, Inc.

*   *   *

Publisher's Cataloging-in-Publication
Fitterling, Thomas.

Thelonious Monk: his life and music / Thomas Fitterling;
translated by Robert Dobbin; foreword by Steve Lacy.
p.   cm.
Translation of *Thelonious Monk: sein Leben, seine Musik, seine
Schallplatten.*
Includes bibliographical references and index.
Includes discography.
Preassigned LCCN: 97-70463
ISBN 0-9653774-1-5

1. Monk, Thelonious. 2. Jazz Musicians–United States–
Biography. I. Title

ML417.M846F58 1997   786.2'165'092
                            QBI97-40270

*   *   *

Photo Credits
Francis Paudras/Jazz Memories: pages 1, 36, 38, 49, 51, 53, 55,
    69, 70, 75, 79, 83
Lee Tanner/The Jazz Image: 2, 18, 62, 65, 77, 120
Francis Wolff/© Mosaic Images: 72, 96, 113
© William P. Gottlieb/Library of Congress: Ira & Leonore
    Gershwin Fund: 29
Corbis-Bettmann: 60
Amalie R. Rothschild/Corbis-Bettman: 103
UPI/Corbis-Bettman: 94
Riccardo Schwamenthal: 43
Don Schlitten: 64
Photo X (right reserved): 24, 80, 106

For

For A. von Streit, a brilliant musician and musicologist, my love and companion;

and Horst Weber, the man responsible for my becoming a jazz writer.

Translator's note

This translation owes much to the co-operation of the author, Thomas Fitterling. He reviewed all the work, and graciously answered questions about many specific passages. His equal facility in German and English saved me from many errors.

ROBERT DOBBIN
Berkeley, January 1997

Preface

THELONIOUS SPHERE MONK. The name immediately strikes us as odd and mysterious. Despite the thorough analysis of his work that began with his belated recognition in the second half of the fifties, and reached new heights after his death in 1982, relatively little is still known about Monk the man. His date of birth, for instance, which had traditionally been given as October 10, 1920, was corrected to the year 1917 only in the early seventies. Thelonious Monk never troubled himself about the matter. It lay outside the realm of one of the few things that interested him, his music. And he divorced himself, quietly but irrevocably, from just about everything else.

His apartment in New York served as a refuge since his childhood until nearly the end of his life—first with his mother, then with his wife, Nellie. Later he was granted the refuge of Baroness Nica de Koenigswarter's estate. These three women treasured him and saw to the external order in his life. At the beginning of his career there was also an enforced inner exile from the business end of jazz. That the Monk household stood open to the restlessly searching young musicians who were prepared to keep the master company on his endless piano excursions, is no contradiction. He did not conform to the world, but he did admit a few people into his own who were willing to adopt it in their turn.

Certainly in the life of this complete individualist there were fewer scandals and affairs than in the lives of most other musicians of the bebop era. This relative lack of sensational material, together with Monk's reserve toward the press, helps account for the fact that, years after his death, there is still little biographical work on him published in English, in contrast to many another pioneer and legends of modern jazz. The first edition of this book, which appeared in 1987, had to reckon with this circumstance. But I received help in its preparation from the late Martin Williams, who sent me precious historic material. Michael Cuscuna's support deserves to be acknowledged here as well. The list of sources in the back of the present edition lists much of the comprehensive material on Monk's life that has begun to appear in recent years.

This revised edition for Berkeley Hills Books will take its place in this growing body of work. New information from the most recent sources has been incorporated, and errors in the earlier edition have, to the best of my ability, been corrected. The basic format of the first edition, which was addressed to a broad range of interested readers, and organized into three sections accordingly, has been retained. The first section gives a concise account of Monk's life. The second analyzes his music. The final section aims to provide a comprehensive discography that includes descriptions and critiques of nearly all the albums and CDs on which Monk plays. There is a catalogue of videos relating to Monk, and a glossary of musical terms that appear in the body of the book.

I trust that this edition will bring the reader closer to the life and work of Thelonious Sphere Monk.

THOMAS FITTERLING
Ulm, December 1996

Contents

Foreword
Steve Lacy

MY FIRST CONTACT WITH MONK'S MUSIC WAS IN NEW YORK, 1953, when I joined Cecil Taylor's quartet. One of the pieces we rehearsed, performed, and recorded was 'Bemsha Swing.'

In '55 Cecil took me to a downtown club to hear Monk's quartet, which included Ernie Henry, Wilbur Ware, and Shadow Wilson. This was a wonderful little group, and I was immediately and completely won over by the high quality of invention of the written material, the spontaneous interplay of the four musicians, and the swinging humor and beauty of Monk's *sound* at the piano. C.T. and I were both mad about Duke Ellington's music, and here we both agreed was the true contemporary continuation of that school.

Soon after that first hearing, I started to collect Thelonious' records and began *trying* to learn some of his compositions on the soprano saxophone. To my glad surprise, I found out that they suited the instrument to a 'T'! I had learned a lot of Charlie Parker's lines, but they were made for alto sax, and were too low for my horn. I had begun on piano (until I heard Tatum!), and then discovered (through Bechet) the soprano sax, and Monk's pieces were just right for me. They were not too high, not too low, not too easy (I didn't yet know how hard they were!), full of interesting rhythmic, melodic, dynamic, harmonic, and structural problems. And nobody was playing them except Thelonious himself. Even he was just performing a small group of them, probably because at that time he was not performing much in public.

The more of his music I learned, the more interesting and challenging it became. On my first LP as a leader, *Soprano Sax* in '57, I recorded a version (full of mistakes) of 'Work.' I was quite proud of it, but later found out that I did not have it down correctly at all. Nonetheless, Monk complimented me on it. (By this time I had gotten to know him a little.) T. was always glad when someone at least tried to play his music. He was also very interested in errors, and when someone made a mistake he would pick up on it and examine the *ramifications* (Duke's word) therein.

By this time Miles Davis' record of "Round Midnight' (written when Monk was 18!) was out and a big hit, and people were getting more and more interested in Monk himself. But still nobody was playing his other compositions—perhaps because there were no publications, and because their originality and complexity made them seem forbidding to most players.

For my second Prestige LP, in '59, I decided to do an all-Thelonious Monk record, *Reflections*. It consisted of seven Monk tunes from the late forties and early fifties. For two years I tried to learn every piece of his on record I could get my hands on (about thirty-five in all), and listened to them over and over until I *thought* I had them down. From all of these I chose seven to record, including some very difficult and interesting numbers, such as 'Skippy' and 'Four in One.' Mal Waldron was my pianist and partner on this project and we began a lifelong collaboration, based on our mutual interest in the music of Monk. We were lucky enough to have Elvin Jones on drums, who understood Thelonious' music perfectly. When the LP came out, T. was very pleased, and I was gratified when he again began to perform 'Ask Me Now', after not having played it for many years.

By this time Monk was playing at the Five Spot with Coltrane, later with Johnny Griffin. I lived around the corner, and was able to attend the nightly unfolding of this marvelous music. In those days the gigs would last six weeks or more, and the price of admission was a bottle of beer. So more and more fans, musicians, famous painters, critics, and writers discovered Monk's music, and followed the action nightly. This was an exciting and unforgettable experience for all of us, wonderful times.

The next year, 1960, Jimmy Giuffre took over my trio (Dennis Charles, Buell Neidlinger), which played all Monk tunes, for an engagement at the Five Spot. Nica (the Baroness de Koenigswarter) brought Thelonious by to hear us perform, and several months later I was engaged to play at the Jazz Gallery, making Monk's quartet into a quintet for a gig that lasted sixteen weeks. During those very intense four months we also performed at several jazz festivals, in New York and Philadelphia (there is a collector's tape of three numbers from that show). We also doubled at the Apollo Theater in Harlem (ten days opposite Miles, Coltrane, Betty Carter, James Moody, 'Moms' Mabley, and a film!)

This gig was one of my most memorable experiences. No rehearsal, just play! Fortunately, I knew most of Monk's melodies (except the very first tune, which I had to bluff). After a few weeks together, the group began to get a *sound.* Monk would only let Charlie Rouse and me play in unison or octaves; he said that was the most difficult to do well, and that if we could do that, it was easy to add harmony parts, or second voices (which he played at the piano). He was right, of course, and the quintet developed a lovely ensemble sound.

Thelonious would not tell me what to play, but he would stop me if I got carried away: 'Don't play all that bullshit, play the melody! Pat your foot and sing the melody in your head, or play off the rhythm of the melody, never mind the so-called chord changes.' Also, 'Don't pick up from me, I'm accompanying *you!*' Also: *'Make the drummer sound good!'* These tips are among the most valuable things anyone has ever told me.

Some of T.'s other bits of wisdom:

'The *inside* of the tune [the bridge] is what makes the *outside* sound good.'

'A genius is the one who is most like himself.'

'It's always night, otherwise you wouldn't need the light!'

'Whatever you think can't be done, someone will come along and do it.'

'Monk = know = 'Always Know' (where you are).'

'When you're swinging, swing some more!'

'You've got to know the importance of discrimination, also the value of what you *don't* play, the use of space, and letting music go by, only picking out certain parts.'

'A note can be as big as a mountain, or small as a pin. It only depends on a musician's imagination.'

I also participated in several versions of Monk's big band, with Thad Jones, Phil Woods, Charlie Rouse, and arrangements by Hall Overton. We played and recorded at Lincoln Center. Hall wrote out and arranged Monk's recorded improvisations on 'Four in One' and several other pieces, so that I was playing T.'s right hand figures, way up above the normal range of the saxophone. When we finally played these arrangements correctly, after much rehearsal, they sounded wonderful, and Monk and everyone else was very happy.

T. saw how anxious I was to take a chorus in this band, and so he gave out the solos to everyone *except* me! This was very frustrating at the time, but later I realized what a valuable lesson in discipline and non-volition he was giving me. Once he told me, 'Never ask for a job, just be on the scene and be ready!' He himself learned the hard way, when they took away his cabaret card and he couldn't work for years in New York, while others were beginning to play his music, and finally correctly.

I think his wife Nellie's contribution to Monk's development was very important. She always believed in his great talent, and supported him during the time he couldn't work, so that he could continue the research he was pursuing at the piano, and in his compositions. Monk was always unique and somewhat isolated. The encouragement and love of musicians like Sonny Rollins (he and I used to practice Monk tunes on the Williamsburg bridge), Coltrane, Dizzy Gillespie, Max Roach, Kenny Clarke, Charlie Mingus, Gil Evans, Nica, and some of the critics and club owners, were vital.

Thelonious was a beautiful man, with a special sense of humor, and a love of play, all sorts of play (music, dance, ping-pong, other sports, and even playing with death and 'playing dead'). When we were working at the Jazz Gallery, it was summertime, and in between sets we would be on the street, in front of the club, and T. would be playing with the passing cars and traffic lights, like a matador with the bulls.

All his music can be sung and swung, and derives fundamentally from, and towards, *dance.* Rhythm and melody were one for him. He told me that when he was young he was excellent at mathematics, and I believed him because his sense of time and space was uncanny. In jazz, and especially after the bebop revolution in the forties (of which Thelonious was the leading strategist), the *mise-en-place* was opened up as a source of new lines, and the rhythmic content was greatly enhanced.

When the gig at the Jazz Gallery was over after the summer of 1960, Monk did not fire me, but he went back to his normal quartet format. Adding me to the group was a daring experiment on his part, but not strictly necessary. I think he knew that I needed that first-hand experience, which I greatly profited from.

We remained very good friends, and I continued to visit him until I left for Europe in '65. I saw him when he made the last tour with Dizzy Gillespie and Art Blakey. He sounded wonderful, but he was disoriented by the geographical violence of that tour

(Stockholm, Rome, Paris, Budapest, London, etc., with no rest or logic). Monk was only comfortable in New York, where he could be coherent.

I was not there when his health broke down, but I visited him at Nica's house a year or two before he died. Thelonious had lost his appetite for everything. He did not touch the piano for the last seven years of his life (I was told). It was heartbreaking to see him like that, but his heart and spirit had taken a lot of hard knocks in his long career. His mind was discouraged and gave up, for a myriad of reasons.

It's about time we had a clear picture of the story of Monk, which Fitterling's interesting study delivers. I am happy to recommend it to anyone interested in the man and his music.

January 1997, Berlin

PART 1

MONK'S LIFE

Beginnings

IN THE LIFE OF THE MATURE THELONIOUS MONK, epochal moments often occurred at or around the same time as a new record deal. One thinks of his marriage and the Blue Note contract in 1947, the birth of his son in December 1949 and the change to the Prestige label, and the death of his mother and birth of his daughter in 1953-54 followed by the change to Riverside the following year. Chance certainly played a role here, but this nevertheless enables us to consider his professional and private life in close conjunction.

First, it is necessary to correct the myths surrounding Monk's birth and name. For a long time the year of his birth had been given as 1920. In 1974, however, Leonard Feather saw Monk's entry in the birth register of Rocky Mount, North Carolina. It reads, 'October 10, 1917, Thelius Monk.' The name is written with an unsteady hand, and can also be read as 'Thelious.' The father's name appears to be 'Thelsious', and the mother's 'Barbra.' The father's profession is given as 'ice puller', his mother's 'household work.' The middle name, 'Sphere', which Monk increasingly came to use, is missing here. Many an author in a flight of fancy has chosen to see the musical development of Thelonious Sphere Monk providentially prefigured in the conjunction of middle and last name: 'The lonely monk in his own sphere', or something of the sort.

According to Ponzio and Postif, the authors of *Blue Monk,* the name 'Thelonious' comes from 'Thelonius,' the Latinized form of the German name 'Tillman.' German missionaries could have brought the name to the Carolinas in the Bible Belt. How ironic that Thelonious Monk, a musician often likened by colleagues and critics to an African shaman or medicine man, should have borne the name of a hero of German epic. As far as the middle name, 'Sphere,' is concerned, Monk's son Thelonious Jr. claims that it was a part of his father's original Christian name, and derived from Monk's maternal grandfather, Sphere Batts. Monk did not learn of this name, however, until the forties, judging from certain documents. From then on he used it as a hip accessory. He would joke that owing to his middle name he could never be called a 'square.'

Of decisive importance for Monk's musical development was an event that took place when he was six. The family, with an ailing father, a strict but strongly devoted mother, two sons, and an older daughter, left North Carolina for New York in search of better fortune. The Monk family was in this respect part of a larger social movement. The year Monk was born, the US entered the First World War, and the economic boom in the north stemming from the war effort precipitated a great migration of the poor and underemployed northward from the southern states. In the south the economic and legal situation of blacks was less affected by the war. Jim Crow laws effectively institutionalized oppression and segregation.

The Monk family did not settle in the heart of Harlem, but nearby, in San Juan Hill. This was then a small and more affluent neighborhood, populated mainly by West Indians, and adjacent to white neighborhoods. The choice of residence would prove significant, as would the fact that Monk's mother found steady employment in the city administration.

The Monk family moved into a small two-bedroom apartment on the ground floor of 263 West 63rd Street, between 10th and 11th (or West End) Avenue. It was directly above the Hudson with its busy docks. Monk's family would live there until 1981. San Juan Hill was an area with a thriving music scene. With her job in the city administration, Monk's mother secured the family a reasonable income. It was the more necessary, since soon the family would lose their father. In order to convalesce he returned to the south, and would not return.

Thelonious was now in elementary school, PS 141. He must have been an especially charming and energetic child. When Engine Company 40 of the New York Fire Department, in accordance with its custom, chose a youth from the neighborhood to be their mascot and protégé, the choice fell on him.

The young Thelonious grew up in a city that, contrary to what many jazz histories report, was already the international capital of jazz. By the end of the nineteenth century, much of the style and tone of life in the United States was set in New York. It remained the artistic, cultural, and economic center of the nation. It was here above all that a change in cultural values was realized, from the old American ethic of hard work and constraint to a new ideal that emphasized pleasure and self-expression as acceptable routes to personal well-being. As symptoms of this change, numerous entertainment centers opened to meet a growing demand for live music. Prohibition in 1920 paradoxically furthered the trend. In New York and Chicago cabarets and speakeasies sprang up. Jazz was the preferred musical accompaniment at these romantic rendezvous. The Cotton Club in Harlem, which Duke Ellington helped make famous, epitomized the New York jazz scene in the twenties. So while in Chicago a distinct form of early jazz had emerged, in New York its development would lead to big-band swing. The evolution of swing, with its large personnel requirements, attracted musicians to the city in increasing numbers.

The invention of radio also had a decisive part in the development of jazz. At the time, there were no satisfactory ways to record music, so radio had a constant need for live performers. The great radio stations, as well as the major concert agencies, were all in New York. The city's role as headquarters for the media and the touring industry was now established, and as the recording industry emerged it also began to take root there. All these factors combined to make it the center of the jazz world.

In this vital atmosphere Monk received his education as a pianist. His sister, Marion, further reports that in their predominantly West Indian neighborhood learning a musical instrument was part of a normal education. She herself was compelled to study piano. Her brother had to learn trumpet, because he refused to learn the violin. But Thelonious had trouble with his lungs, and because he was already capable of picking out melodies on the piano (which a friend of the family had given them) he began to take the lessons that his sister wanted to avoid. The lessons do not appear to have been extensive. Monk would later claim that he had been fascinated by the piano's mechanism for producing sound, that he felt that something 'right' should be done with it, and that he taught himself to play. His mother supported him in this direction. 'My mother never imagined that I would do anything else; she always supported me. When I wanted to become a jazz musician, she had nothing against it.' Considering that this was during a boom era for jazz musicians, hers was a not uncommonly liberal attitude.

At fourteen, Monk played regularly at rent parties in the neighborhood. These were parties to which the neighbors were invited, who, through their financial contribution in consideration of musical entertainment, would help meet the rent of the not-quite-liquid host. Besides this, he accompanied his mother on piano and organ when she sang in St. Cyprian's Baptist Church. (When she later converted to the Jehovah's Witnesses, she also brought her son Thomas, a prizefighter and policeman three years younger than Thelonious, to the faith.)

Monk was now of high school age. At Peter Stuyvesant High School he distinguished himself in mathematics, physics, and basketball. His interest in jazz was also clearly marked. Initially it centered on the work of Louis Armstrong and Duke Ellington, then on Fats Waller, Earl Hines, and especially James P. Johnson, who lived in the neighborhood and was a local hero. When Art Tatum came to New York in 1932, he became for Thelonious 'the greatest pianist I had ever heard.'

Every Wednesday at the Apollo, the famous Harlem palace of music, an amateur talent contest was held. Monk, who at this time played in a rather simple stride style, reports that he won this competition so often that he was finally debarred from further participation. After the end of Prohibition he earned pocket money during summer vacations playing background music with a trio in a Harlem bar-and-grill. Social and economic conditions by now had changed. The consequences of the Depression that began in 1929, along with the lapse of Prohibition, undermined the social structure of the community. Crime was on the rise and hard drugs appeared, making life a struggle for many.

As 1933 came to an end, Monk made the decisive leap to professional musician. His success competing at the Apollo encouraged his decision. He left high school early, at the age of sixteen, to make a cross-country tour with a female evangelist who also performed as a miracle healer. For two years Monk was separated from his home and family. This period contributed greatly to his development as a man and a musician. In the evangelist's band, besides Monk, there was a trumpeter, a saxophonist and a percussionist. According to Monk's account, the band played a type of rock 'n' roll, or rhythm and blues, to accompany the recitation of religious texts.

Thelonious (right), with brother Thomas and sister Marion in New York

In the cities in which the troupe appeared Monk sought entry to the local jazz scene in late-night jam sessions. Kansas City was one important stop. The government of Kansas City was acknowledged to be corrupt—involved in illegal entertainment activities such as gambling. But by virtue of city collusion, there was a boom in the arts and entertainment that had not been seen since before the Depression. The best jazz musicians were attracted to the city. In wide-open jam sessions they developed an ensemble style marked by rhythmic fluency and the frequent use of solo improvisation and riffs. It was represented first by Benny Moten, then by Count Basie's band with Lester Young, later still by the band of Jay McShann with Charlie Parker. Drummer Kenny Clarke and pianist Mary Lou Williams were also in the city.

Mary Lou Williams was deeply impressed by Monk when they first met. She would later report that, although he made use of other pianistic techniques, he already played in what would become his unmistakable style. She also stresses that the innovative harmonies so characteristic of him were already in evidence. Emboldened by the friendliness of this older colleague, Monk entrusted her with his artistic credo: He meant to create something new; it annoyed him no end, he said, to hear musicians always playing the same things in the same manner.

In 1936 he was back in New York with his mother and family. With various odd jobs that escaped the scrutiny of the powerful music union, he made a modest living performing in dance halls and pubs.

According to the address that was delivered at Monk's funeral service, Monk at this time took classes in harmony and arrangement at the Juilliard School of Music. This cannot be corroborated by other sources, however. And it contradicts the testimony of Monk himself, who always emphasized that he was self-taught, and only reluctantly owned up to the piano lessons he took as a child. Laurent de Wilde, in his French biography of Monk, tracks down what he calls the 'Juilliard legend.' He finds no support for it, and believes it stems from the fact that much later, in 1958-59, Monk collaborated with Juilliard instructor Overton Hall on big-band arrangements, and often visited the famous school in this man's company.

The public at this time favored the 'sweet music' of the pre-dominantly white big bands whose swing melodies became the soundtrack of the New Deal. The role of the radio in keeping the masses entertained cannot be overestimated. Black musicians shared to some degree in this boom, but they did so at the cost of renouncing their musical roots. In response, young black musicians increasingly met among themselves after hours to work out their distinctive ideas. In the abundant free time he enjoyed, Monk worked on his own musical plans. With his striving for innovation he was actually typical of a generation of African-American musicians. Shaped by the urban life of northern American cities, better educated and more self-conscious than their parents, they looked upon jazz as their cultural heritage and were convinced of the need for a renewal of their music—a renewal of what, by rights, belonged to them already.

Kenny Clarke, who often met with Monk at this time, is representative of his generation. While in Teddy Hill's famous big band he was on the way to developing the modern style of drum playing, with its open beat and contrapuntal accent. The trumpeter and pianist Denzil Best (who later switched to drums for reasons of health) also belongs to the group, and last but not least Dizzy Gillespie, who had played with Teddy Hill, too. A highly talented teenage pianist, seven years Monk's junior, by the name of Bud Powell was from the same neighborhood as Monk, and one of his closest friends. Now Monk was increasingly playing as a full-time jazz pianist with the Duke Ellington trumpeter Cootie

Williams and others. At this time Williams hired the young Powell, and recorded "Round Midnight' with him, to which Williams contributed his own introduction. After Bernie Hanigen added lyrics, a confusing composer credit appeared on many records, reading: 'B. Hanigen, T. Monk, C. Williams.'

This loose group of friends and musicians from a younger generation found its point of meeting and crystallization when Henry Minton, an older musician and one of the first black jazz entrepreneurs, undertook to make a modern neighborhood social center and jazz club out of a somewhat dilapidated wing of the Cecil Hotel, at 210 West 118th Street in Harlem. Young musicians with new ideas were given the opportunity to try them out before an audience.

Minton's idea was to reproduce the kind of music scene that had flourished a few years before in Kansas City. Early in 1941 he engaged Teddy Hill as manager for this new locale, which he dubbed Minton's Playhouse. Hill in the meantime had dissolved his big band. But he wanted to do something for the people who had worked with him, and he had an idea. In the afternoon Minton's would be a neighborhood social center with a well-stocked jukebox. In the evening there would be good, cheap food. Later, at night, it would attract up-and-coming musicians with an excellent in-house rhythm section with whom they could jam for free. On Monday, 'Celebrity Night,' dinner would be offered *gratis* to the established musicians as an inducement for them to sit in.

The choice of rhythm section determined the music that would develop at Minton's. For the original band, Teddy Hill called upon the avant-garde drummer Kenny Clarke—whom he had actually fired a few years before because his unorthodox accents threw the musicians into confusion. For pianist, Teddy Hill originally wanted Sonny White, the pianist in his old band. But White was unavailable. Instead, Monk got the job. By this time he had become a quiet minimalist at the piano. His harmonic conceptions had already exercised considerable influence on his circle of friends. In Minton's band, Monk and Clarke had a secure, long-term contract. The Minton's Playhouse adventure could begin.

Monk with Howard McGhee, Roy Eldridge, and Teddy Hill,
at the entrance to Minton's Playhouse

The Eye of the Bebop Hurricane

SURELY NO JAZZ CLUB WOULD MAKE SUCH ENDURING HISTORY AS Minton's Playhouse. This informal meeting place opened its doors at exactly the right time and place. New York had become the desired destination of established bands, as well as home to striving young musicians who lived in the Harlem neighborhood. Many of them were resentful because the entertainment industry favored white swing stars, while they themselves remained shut out of the wider American market. Among these musicians there was an awareness that the true innovators of this popular music had been black, and that jazz belonged to them as their cultural heritage. They wanted to make music that, economically speaking, would belong to them alone and this time would not be taken away from them so easily. Thus a youth movement developed and announced its claim to leadership. From the start, Minton's had the right booking policy with which to wage this battle for position. Since it was located in Harlem, it served as a daily meeting place for local musicians who would congregate and, outside the usual jam sessions, develop theoretical concepts in their afternoon get-togethers.

Thelonious Monk, along with Kenny Clarke, was the quiet center of this activity. Dizzy Gillespie gradually penetrated the circle, as did the trumpeter Joe Guy and guitarist Charlie Christian. Christian had played with Benny Goodman, and on his electrified instrument had already revolutionized the playing of the guitar with his single note lines. He bought another amplifier especially for Minton's; it stood ready for him whenever he dropped by on his way from the Goodman gig. Tenor saxophonist Don Byas regularly visited, as did the young Art Blakey and bassist Jimmy Blanton, who had introduced the four-to-the-bar walking bass style to the Ellington band.

Increasingly, one also saw musicians of the older generation at Minton's who sensed a challenge. Often, though, they had to admit defeat when trying to improvise over tunes they thought they knew, since at Minton's, these tunes were blithely subjected to delirious tempos and radical new harmonization. This was the initial experience of both Roy Eldridge and Lester Young, the established stars on trumpet and saxophone. But, challenged and provoked, they would return. Coleman Hawkins, the great father figure of the tenor sax, was almost in hiding after his return from Europe. But he was an unqualified admirer of the new music, and later would enlist young beboppers—Monk in particular—for his recordings. The pianist and orchestra leader Earl Hines, whose career took many unexpected turns, was another frequent guest at Minton's.

The musical nucleus, or the 'eye of the bebop hurricane' at Minton's, was the team of Kenny Clarke and Thelonious Monk. Both had developed their personal style to the greatest extent by the time Minton's opened. They laid the rhythmic and harmonic foundation of the new style, as Dizzy Gillespie attests in his autobiography. Gillespie reports how much he learned from Monk in his search for a way to express his own musical ideas—Monk, with his oblique chord changes, his use of the flatted fifth, his ninth chords, and his way of arriving at harmonic resolutions by way of hitherto untried intermediate passages.

Gillespie and Charlie Christian were interested in cultivating a new rhythmic and harmonic virtuosity. They had been suitably impressed by the young alto saxophonist Charlie Parker when he first came to New York in 1939 with the Kansas City band of Jay McShann. His musical search seemed to be leading him in the same direction. A year after Minton's opened, Charlie Parker returned to New York on a freight train, and was now playing in Clark Monroe's Uptown House, Harlem's other jam-session club. It was on 138th Street, and was popular above all with the musicians of Count Basie's circle from Kansas City.

Kenny Clarke, and later Dizzy Gillespie, recognized in Parker a new force on the scene. They felt a strong spiritual kinship with him, and persuaded him to collaborate in the Minton enterprise. Now, in 1942, every instrument in the composition of a classic jazz quintet had a pioneering representative in the Minton circle. Clarke, as the oldest and most respected of the boppers, was nominally the leader of the band. With his easy and natural authority, he saw to it that the outward eccentricities cultivated by so many band members did not jeopardize their joint adventure. The house pianist, it must be said, was a difficult case. Fundamentally spoiled by his doting mother, Thelonious Monk arrived late more and more often, and regarded it as his job to be unreliable. At the same time his goatee, sunglasses, and black beret—the prototype of his notorious and constantly changing headgear—came to identify the bopper image, at the same time expressing his subversive, anti-establishment outlook.

Taciturn and apparently shut off from others, Monk gradually adopted an idiosyncratic lifestyle, of which the regular consumption of alcohol already played a part. John Carisi, the composer and trumpeter who played in Miles Davis' Capitol orchestra, reports that Monk once said to him, 'What? You want to be a jazzman and you don't drink?' Kenny Clarke reports that, after closing time once, they went to the subway together, whereupon Monk took his leave, and—dead-drunk but steady—walked directly over the tracks to the opposite platform. He certainly helped himself to drugs at this time too as part of his daily dose of stimulation.

Two decades later, in 1964, the famous *Time* article states: 'Every day is a brand-new pharmaceutical event for Monk: alcohol, dexedrine, sleeping potions, whatever is at hand, charge through his bloodstream in baffling combinations. Predictably, Monk is highly unpredictable.'

This is a delicate subject, that has been taboo for some jazz writers and musicians. A statement like the one made by the expatriate Mal Waldron on the occasion of his seventieth birthday is all the more welcome for its candor: 'The jazz scene was a cutthroat rat race then. The musicians were exposed to tremendous pressure and resorted to various crutches. Hard drugs were the most widespread ones. They dominated the scene; without being addicted, access to the important inner circles was denied. Some record companies and club owners would only hire junkies. With them they could be sure they wouldn't insist on their rights. Outside the clubs the police treated all black musicians as junkies anyway, so why not have the have the game if you got the blame?'

In his free time, Monk would wander in a musical odyssey from club to club, and install himself unannounced, when the mood hit him, at the houses of friends, in order to sit down at the piano unencumbered by time and place. Again, he would sleep whenever the rhythm of his life called for it–at home, with friends, at Minton's, and at Minton's sometimes during a gig. He was less interested in the bravura aspects of the new music and more in the compositional aspects, which is why his enthusiasm for Charlie Parker was more muted than that of his colleagues. He not only re-harmonized old standards, but wrote new pieces with new harmonies. Thus themes emerged that immediately became part of the standard bop repertoire, such as ''Round Midnight' and 'Epistrophy.' More and more he invited musicians to his house to demonstrate his ideas, quietly and patiently, at the piano.

Bud Powell was among Monk's most frequent guests, and a frequent host when Monk wandered off in search of a piano to play. They were friends for life, and Powell remained an enthusiastic interpreter of Monk's music—despite the fact that his piano style, modeled on the right hand 'horn-lines' of Charlie Parker and Dizzy Gillespie, was the dead opposite of Monk's style of play. For many critics and musicians, Powell, with his brilliantly fast and fluent technique, became the true representative of the bebop piano. Ironically, the beboppers at Minton's allowed Bud Powell to come aboard only at Monk's insistence.

During the years of the Second World War, a shift in popular musical tastes resulted in the closing of the grand dance palaces and the dissolution of the big bands. Increasingly, smaller venues came into vogue, developing after the war into what now are customarily called jazz clubs. A twenty-percent entertainment tax was imposed on dance events in New York with live music. Dance clubs dropped in popularity, and the purveyors of the big band sound suffered accordingly. Musicians lacked steady employment with stable bands, and increasingly worked on their own account. This led to the formation of insulated groups of jazz performers in which everyone was a potential leader, expected to engage his friends as sidemen. Whoever belonged to the clique got a job, and with it, the potential for national and international attention. Jam sessions acquired a new function: they became initiation rituals, 'cutting sessions', in which new recruits played their way into the inner circle. Monk, a radical individualist both as a man and musician, fit into this context only in part. Notoriously, he declined to roll out the red carpet for the soloists he accompanied. When he played, everyone else had to play his way too.

Bebop was finally gaining an audience outside Harlem. Its appearance on 52nd Street at such clubs as the Onyx and the 3 Deuces marked the first step in its progress toward the white intellectual 'downtown', south of Harlem. Downtown was becoming the center of the New York jazz scene, where all the great stars of the late swing area appeared in clubs. In August of 1943 Dizzy

Gillespie performed at the Onyx, in a bebop combo to which Lester Young, the bassist Oscar Pettiford, drummer Max Roach, and initially Monk, also belonged. Later Monk would be replaced by George Wallington, who was more punctual and didn't unsettle the soloists with his own queer ideas of accompaniment. Monk in any case did not like to play outside Harlem. He was afraid that the commercial world of music would again rob the creators of the new style of their music, as it had once robbed the fathers of swing.

While the attraction of downtown New York grew, the loosely constructed fabric of Minton's slowly unraveled. Jam sessions took place only on Mondays, and on the remaining weekdays regular bands alternated. Monk was able to work there only sporadically now. And owing to his personal and musical oddities, he seldom got work elsewhere. Another circumstance added to his troubles. The radio stations to this point had relied on live music for their programming. But at the beginning of the forties, recording techniques had evolved to the point where station managers could dispense with live music altogether.

The musical community, having lost a significant source of income, reacted by refusing to record. This was the so-called 'Great Ban' which lasted from 1942 to 1944, when musical recordings were made only under the auspices of the military. The record companies were forced to share with the musicians the royalties they got when their product was played on the radio. This should be borne in mind when one is tempted to lament the fact that, owing to the ban, the development of jazz during this period is not better documented, and that the public at the time remained largely unaware of its direction.

The public responded with all the more alarm when suddenly confronted after the war with the new style of jazz. Contributing to its alarm was the sense that a new black self-awareness was emerging, stimulated, in turn, by consciousness of the signal contribution black Americans had made to the victory overseas. The new music, although not widely heard, was not entirely unknown to, or unsuccessful with, the public. It made its way into the thriving jazz clubs that were opening up on 52nd Street in midtown, if only after a delay.

One of the few people who hired Monk on a regular basis was the old master Coleman Hawkins. Monk would always be grateful to him for this. In his successful later years, it would be he who hired Hawkins. And when the saxophonist lay dying in 1969, Monk took the trouble to look after him. In 1944 Hawkins engaged Monk for his band, alongside Don Byas on second tenor, trumpeter Benny Harris, and Denzil Best on drums. With Monk (but without Byas and Harris) he then entered the studio, producing the first official recordings of Thelonious Monk, *Bean and the Boys*. Monk was also on hand when the Hawkins band appeared at the Onyx club. Hawkins' appreciation of Monk had its limits, however. 'Some of the most awful things that I ever had to en-

The Onyx Club, New York 1944. Coleman Hawkins (ts) with Benny Harris (tp), Don Byas (ts), Monk, Denzil Best (d) and Eddie Robinson (b)

dure, I endured on Monk's account,' Hawkins would later report. 'Every night I asked myself why I didn't get a normal pianist for the band.'

One critic, at least, recognized Monk's uniqueness, Herbie Nichols. As a pianist he was as much a well-kept secret during his lifetime as Monk was in his early years. He also wrote about jazz, and in *Music Dial* he praised the involved rhythmic structure of Monk's 'magnificent melodic lines.' An increasing number of musicians, in fact, were now performing Monk compositions. But in accordance with the practice of the jazz community at the time, they would claim author or co-author rights. In any case, though he continued to help out in one or another band, Monk found little steady work or recognition as a pianist. His difficulties were compounded by the fact that he strictly refused to make compromises in his music, or accept distasteful jobs solely for commercial reasons. And precisely because of its exotic character, bebop did have some commercial appeal. But it would not be until the next decade that intellectuals who identified themselves as the 'Beat Generation' (after the model of the 'Lost Generation') would make it really fashionable.

Now and again Monk did manage to land a job. On January 21, 1945, he got a welcome gig with Max Roach in Philadelphia. As the musicians were packing up their instruments after the show, the police stormed the club and went after Monk. He refused to show them his identification, and was forcibly arrested. A fan barred the door and challenged the officers. They tried to push him aside, but he wouldn't budge. 'Stop,' he yelled, 'you don't know what you're doing. You're mistreating the greatest pianist in the world!' At this point a nightstick came down on his head like a lightning bolt. The young fan was Monk's best friend, Bud Powell. He was dragged off along with Monk, and thrown into jail after his injury was superficially treated at a hospital.

Monk and Bud Powell in 1964

After his release Powell complained of alarming headaches. He eventually checked into Bellevue Hospital, then spent three months in Creedmore Hospital. There he was treated with various psychoactive drugs and shock therapy. His artistic career had barely started, but henceforth would be bedevilled by psychological problems. Monk was well aware that Powell's intervention had saved him from a similar fate. For his ill-starred protégé he wrote 'In Walked Bud', '52nd Street Theme', and 'Broadway Theme', otherwise known simply as 'The Theme.' The latter pair were intended to be Bud's property alone, and Monk never recorded them.

At the end of 1945, Monk participated in a musical event that made jazz history, though it did not boost his popularity much. The Coleman Hawkins quartet, of which he was then a member, took part in the first of the great touring vehicles organized by Norman Granz. It had its premiere performance on November 26 at Philharmonic Hall in Los Angeles. This series evolved into the legendary musical event, Jazz at the Philharmonic.

But the number of Monk's dates was small in comparison with the success that certain of his former Minton's colleagues were enjoying. Among his friends he admitted that he was bitter that Dizzy Gillespie and Charlie Parker got all the credit for the new music, while he was overlooked. 'If they are going to claim this style for themselves and get all the success and recognition, I'll create another new style for myself, and forge ahead with my own music.' Thus Monk was heard to say, according to saxophonist Budd Johnson, who attended Monk's 'house seminars.'

Monk would interest young musicians in his compositions simply by playing them patiently and deliberately. His mother would meanwhile see to it that the guests got something to eat and drink. The result was that Monk got the chance to perform his music, with its distinctive themes, in an intimate ensemble setting. Sonny Rollins belonged to this private circle, and the young Miles Davis, while visiting New York in 1945, likewise frequented Monk's home. Years later he stated that his progress would not have been as fast without his exposure to Monk.

Yet before Monk finally got the chance to make his own recordings as a band leader, a stint with Dizzy Gillespie's big band helped him to get recognized as a composer. Early in 1946 Gillespie undertook to translate bebop into a big band setting. He hired Gil Fuller as the arranger. Fuller and Gillespie were greatly interested in Monk's originals. After tryouts with Monk's protégé Bud Powell foundered due to his psychological problems, Monk became the pianist in the orchestra. What is less well known is that Monk also took charge of arranging his own compositions. He found arranging for a big band to be tedious work, although later he would take some pleasure in preparing arrangements for smaller groups. Kenny Clarke became Gillespie's drummer after his term of military duty in Europe was over. While in the army and serving at Normandy, Clarke had gotten to know the pianist and arranger John Lewis. He recommended him now to Gillespie, who hired him as arranger of the compositions not written by Monk.

Monk's attitude to work was more professional than Bud Powell's. But he was unpunctual on principle, and Gillespie grew more and more tired with him. When Monk—this time with Kenny Clarke—arrived late for an appearance once again, the orchestra had already begun to play. John Lewis was substituting on piano, and vibraphonist Milt Jackson had taken over the drums. Fortunately for Clarke, Gillespie was still waiting in the wings and couldn't see the drummer, so Clarke unobtrusively managed to relieve Jackson of the drumming duties. Monk was less fortunate. He was fired on the spot.

John Lewis got Monk's job, much to Gil Fuller's chagrin. This incident marked, if not the birth, then the moment of conception, of one of the most successful units in modern jazz: Milt Jackson, John Lewis, Kenny Clarke, and bassist Ray Brown were the founding members of the Modern Jazz Quartet. The fact that Monk was replaced by John Lewis negated a beautiful if speculative dream, that of a quite different Modern Jazz Quartet, one whose outlines can be discerned in the occasional collaboration of Monk with Milt Jackson and Kenny Clarke.

The Blue Note Years
Bright Prospects

AT THE BEGINNING OF 1947, Dizzy Gillespie, Monk's exact contemporary, was a celebrated star on trumpet. Charlie Parker, three year's Monk's junior, was the hero of a growing cult of genius. Both Parker and Gillespie could already look back on an impressive body of recordings. Monk, it is true, was known among insiders as a composer, owing to the performances and appearances of Gillespie's bands and Parker's combos, both of which had several Monk numbers in their repertoire. But with the exception of the 1944 recordings with Coleman Hawkins, which were hard to get hold of, his playing was not officially represented on record.

Now, at the end of his twenties, Thelonious Monk's opportunity seemed to have arrived. The independent record company, Blue Note, decided to sign him. The firm had been founded in 1939 by Alfred Lion, an immigrant from Berlin. His friend Frank Wolff, also a refugee from Nazi Germany, joined on the same year. Their program favored modern swing combos especially. In 1945 and '46 they had considerable success with the Ike Quebec Swingtet. But Quebec was friendly with the modern pianists Bud Powell, Tadd Dameron, and Thelonious Monk. In Monk especially, Quebec had an unshakable faith, and he succeeded in getting Wolff and Lion to share it.

With the enthusiasm born of a new beginning—an enthusiasm also shared by Lion's wife, Lorraine—they undertook to promote Monk. They sold him as 'the high priest of bebop, the mysterious and legendary figure who is responsible for the entire new trend in music; the genius behind the entire movement.' Monk was personally opposed to this crass advertising campaign. He modestly insisted that he had only played at Minton's, he hadn't given lessons. Nevertheless, his name now began to appear in the trade press with some frequency. William Gottlieb, Ira Peck, George Simon, and Orrin Keepnews all wrote features about him.

The bright prospects that opened before Monk led to an important change in his life. Always the shy mumbler, who knew only his private way of life, he now had the confidence to ask a young woman from the neighborhood named Nellie Smith to marry him. An unspoken, mutual affection had existed between them from their playground days. Nellie made sacrifices for Monk, whom she idolized. She would light his cigarettes and silently hand them to him when he was lost in his thoughts. She took care to bring order into his apartment, doing his laundry, and washing his dishes. It was Nellie's unconditional willingness to take charge of Monk's domestic affairs and become a second mother to him that induced Monk to regard marriage with her as natural and attractive.

Monk's home was still on West 63rd Street in San Juan Hill, as it had been since childhood. The region was now deteriorating, owing in part to their proximity to the docks, which were in a long decline. The apartment was dominated by a combination living room/kitchen, with a very 'lived-in' look. The centerpiece of the room was the Steinway grand that Monk leased. Over the piano hung a photo of Dizzy Gillespie with his personal dedication; on the ceiling there was a photo of Billie Holiday. Sources report that the piano was often covered with dirty dishes. Francis Paudras, in his book *La danse des Infidèles* recounts a surprise visit he and Bud Powell paid on Monk. Monk greeted them at the door with the cryptic invitation, 'Come in. I'm going to make the plane for you.' He led them into the main room, and sat himself

Monk and Nellie in 1961 while on tour in Europe

at the piano, at that time supporting about a week's worth of dishes. He then depressed both pedals, and played a chord with all ten fingers. The sonic vibrations set the plates to rattling, and, according to Paudras, produced a sound exactly resembling that of a squadron of fighter planes roaring overhead.

The combination kitchen and living room led into two other rooms, one of which was Monk's hideaway. This refuge was the privilege granted Monk by his mother, since the apartment, besides his wife and mother, was shared by Monk's sister, Marion, her husband, and a nephew. The family ties were strong, and Monk's brother, Thomas, also lived in the neighborhood. Thelonious and Nellie's bedroom had only one small window that looked out on a courtyard in the rear. In this setting Monk spent most of his time during the following years.

Widespread success would not come with the Blue Note

records. They sold only in Harlem and the neighborhoods of northern Manhattan. Still, Lorraine Lion did what she could to make Monk better known downtown as well. She persuaded Max Gordon, owner of the legendary club, The Village Vanguard, to engage Monk. But this guest appearance was a financial disaster. The intellectuals in Greenwich Village sneered at what they considered Monk's primitive technique.

The limited sales of Monk's early records may be partly due to the fact that Blue Note, a progressive company in other respects, was still clinging to the 78 RPM format, whereas larger companies had already made the transition to 33 1/3 RPM. Another reason may be that Monk's records were simply ahead of their time. In any case, they did not conform to the expectations created by advertising Monk as the father of bebop. With his preference for moderate and slow tempos, and his insistence on the carefully crafted composition, Monk was never a typical bebopper.

Considered on their own terms the Blue Note records are difficult to fault, being among the best of Monk's career. Fresh and hungry for recognition, he was finally able to commit to the medium of records his own new music without compromise, and with a group of musicians trained by him personally. His efforts, however, went largely unnoticed. In the annual Reader's Poll of 1948 conducted by the jazz journal *Down Beat*, Monk received a grand total of twenty-three votes for best jazz pianist. At the beginning of the same year, he had a prolonged guest spot at Minton's with the musicians who were already on Blue Note. He also played a concert at New York's famous Town Hall. But the opportunities he had to appear in his native city were becoming fewer and fewer. In August he was found in possession of marijuana and spent thirty days in jail. He also lost his cabaret card for a year. Without it he could not appear in clubs where alcohol was served.

In March of 1949 Monk reluctantly performed outside New York City, in Chicago's Hotel Pershing, and with no great success. On August 31 of that year he was on hand for the opening of the legendary jazz club, Birdland. Typically, he ignored the nervous requests of the owner, Oscar Goodstein, to please not put his glass on top of the brand new piano, and not rest his burning cigarette on the keys. Monk made fun of these admonitions, which shows how difficult he could be, but also shows, incidentally, how he conceived of the piano as a work space, an instrument in the true sense, to be subjected to his will and needs—and no one had better cross him in the process. During another gig he suddenly disappeared under the piano and tore at the pedal bracket, because the rods connected to the pedals were not working properly. None of these things were calculated to make managers enthusiastic about hiring him. The Reader's Poll in *Down Beat* that year reflects his commercial nadir in no uncertain terms: he did not get a single vote.

Monk's popularity, if one can speak of such a thing, did not decline in isolation. The music with which he was generally identified was headed the same way. For the young members of the straitlaced middle class, Cool Jazz or West Coast Jazz, regarded by many as a white version of bebop, or the New Orleans revival, were the genres of music they now identified with. Genuine bebop became increasingly marginalized. As art music, it did not command a large following even in the African-American community, where youth identified with rhythm and blues issued on such labels as Aladdin and Chess.

Outwardly Monk did not allow himself to appear embittered. He holed up in his apartment, playing the piano for even longer stretches of time, or just listened to records. His wife tried to shield him from all unpleasantness, and with various domestic jobs she contrived to keep the household together.

With the arrival of 1950 came new cares and prospects. On December 27, 1949 his son, Thelonious Jr., was born. He was soon known within the family as 'Tootie', after the Disney comic character 'Little Tootie the Tugboat', which Thelonious Jr. could imitate before he could talk. In the new year, Norman Granz, organizer of the 'Jazz at the Philharmonic' series, engaged Monk for an all-star recording, for which he again brought together Charlie Parker and Dizzy Gillespie, for his own Clef (later Verve) label. Bassist Curley Russell and star drummer Buddy Rich completed the group.

But the following year a disastrous incident occurred that put an end to Monk's live performance career in New York for six years. Together with his friend Bud Powell (now addicted to drugs), and other acquaintances, he was stopped by the New York police for a vehicle inspection. Powell shoved him a heroin packet to be stowed in the front seat or thrown out the window. Monk was caught holding the packet. While the other passengers got off lightly, Monk had to spend sixty days behind bars because he refused to implicate his friends. When Nellie reproached him for this, he would only say cryptically, 'I have to be able to walk the streets when I get out.' Worse even than the term in custody was the loss of his city police work permit, or 'cabaret card'—this time for a long period, because it was his second offense. Not until 1957, after intensive efforts and with the help of influential friends, would Monk again appear on the stage of a New York jazz club.

In May 1952, Monk led a band into the studio for the last time with Blue Note. We might just note here a curiosity of his recording routine. At home, he would play through his compositions for hours at a time in the company of his musician friends. But he steadfastly refused to prepare them for recording sessions. They came into the studio and had to interpret the selections fresh, without even knowing beforehand what they were about to play.

Often he would not hand out music, preferring that the participants learn the music by ear, which he felt required a more profound level of familiarity. He was opposed to recording second takes, much less third ones. He believed that with every additional take the essential mood of the piece was diminished. When asked in an interview with *Down Beat*, 'Which do you prefer, recording live, or in a studio?', he answered, 'I guess live is better. You have to do it all at one time. Do it the first time, and it's usually best. If you record it over and over again, it's generally a waste of time.'

The Prestige Years
Turning Points

THE PRESTIGE LABEL, for which Bob Weinstock and critic Ira Gitler produced, had a philosophy similar to Blue Note's, in that recording sessions tended to have the character of jam sessions instead of heavily prepared productions with elaborate arrangements. One important difference was that Blue Note often allowed the musicians a day to meet in the studio and rehearse. At Prestige, on the other hand, even this extra expense was avoided. This hardly conflicted with Monk's own attitude toward recording, however. Blue Note, moreover, paid by check, whereas Prestige was known to pay musicians cash in hand immediately following the sessions. This made them especially popular with musicians who were addicted to drugs—and that meant just about all the leading innovators of the time. When Monk's contract with Blue Note expired in 1952, and an offer was made by Prestige, Monk did not hesitate to accept it. Blue Note, for their part, did nothing to try and stop him.

Prestige had the new star of jazz, Miles Davis, under contract, and the Modern Jazz Quartet would soon follow. In these professional circumstances, the less well-known Thelonious Monk, with his reputation for eccentricity, was treated with a certain coolness, especially by Bob Weinstock. The best piano was not at his disposal; the instrument that he plays on his second recording session is clearly out of tune. In his two years at Prestige he spent a grand total of five days in the studio as a leader. He was em-

Monk with Charlie Parker at The Open Door in New York, 1953

ployed as a sideman in the studio for only two. One was with Sonny Rollins, an ardent participant in Monk's 'house seminars.' The other was Christmas Eve 1954, and was, fortunately, the occasion of the legendary recording of 'Bags' Groove' with the all-star band under Miles Davis.

Monk had as much time as he liked to indulge the strange rhythms of his life, playing the piano for hours at a stretch, listening to records, sleeping, or playing with his son. A welcome change was provided by the all-star jam sessions that took place Sunday afternoons at Bob Reisner's Open Door. Bebop greats like Charlie Mingus, Roy Haynes, and Charlie Parker sat in. Unfortunately these gatherings are documented only in photos, not on record. Monk's 'house seminars' played an important role in this period of reduced professional activity. New regulars included the pianists Elmo Hope and Herbie Nichols.

At the end of 1953 the French pianist Henri Renaud came to New York and stayed with George Wallington. Soon he too was one of Monk's 'house seminarians.' He reports how, while there, he tried to work out difficult passages from Monk's ten-inch Prestige LPs. Monk would sit next to him on the couch, and without even looking at the piano would dictate the notes to him perfectly. Ten years earlier Bud Powell had sat on the same piano bench and learned Monk's compositions the same way.

From time to time Henri Renaud would accompany Monk to Tony's Café in Brooklyn. There, without altering his distinctive style—but still with complete success—Monk played dance music for young couples. He was sometimes accompanied on these outings by Sonny Rollins. Despite such occasional gigs, Monk's financial situation was seriously strained. While out on his strolls he would stoop to pick up empty bottles in order to redeem the deposit.

In 1954 his mother died. For nearly four decades she had been the most important person in his life. Monk felt he had not realized the expectations implicit in his mother's devotion. One can imagine how depressed this must have made him. His enforced separation from his family during his relatively brief jail term had already done him psychological damage. Now it became more and more evident how seemingly helpless he was with respect to the everyday details of life. Unable to perform at jazz clubs, and with sales of his records languishing, he had to wrestle with feelings of failure. He was particularly anxious about providing for his young family. That anxiety heightened when his daughter was born on September 5, 1953. She was named 'Barbara' after Monk's mother, but he called her 'Boo Boo' instead. The two had an especially close relationship. Thelonious Jr. speaks of an unspoken but complete mutual understanding between them—an understanding he himself did not share.

Monk was now lapsing into depression more and more often.

At Birdland in New York, 1954: Art Blakey, Duke Jordan, Monk, Henri and Ny Renaud

In Charlotte Zwerin's film *Straight, No Chaser,* Thelonious Jr. gives a frightening description of the bouts of depression in his life, which would regularly occur once or twice a year. 'Things that people would do to him, he would just internalize them, and they would manifest in tremendous fits of depression and euphoria, a very schizophrenic type of thing. And when this would happen—on certain occasions we had to hospitalize him—he would generally close up, introvert, and then he would get excited and may pace for three or four days, and eventually he would get exhausted. It was hard to say how it moved ... It is a startling thing when you look your father in the eye, and he doesn't know who you are ... But my mother clearly let me know that it was our responsibility to look out for this guy the way he looked out for us every minute he was able.'

When he was OK, he was the self-sacrificing father, with whom the children would lie in bed for hours at a time, playing endless games of cards; or who would teach his son in the kitchen the tricks of playing basketball. It is difficult to credit this talent for sports to such a figure, but in fact it is interesting to note that Monk repeatedly won the New York Musicians' ping-pong championship.

In a different, and happier respect, 1954 marked a turning point in Monk's life. He had once mentioned to his guest Henri Renaud that he was curious to know how jazz was received on the other side of the ocean. Renaud telephoned Charles Delaunay and a place was found for Monk at the Parisian 'Salon du Jazz 1954.' There he played with European musicians, who struggled with his music. In typical fashion, he had not rehearsed them. Even if he had, it probably would not have helped much. Monk had to appear with the star of French Dixieland, Claude Luter, at this time a regular pop idol, but a very uncongenial partner. The concert was a failure. Nevertheless, the French jazz press honored him with many front covers and articles, and the French label

Backstage, Paris 1954

Swing (later Vogue) made a solo record with him. This relaxed atmosphere resulted in one of Monk's most beautiful solo recordings.

Behind this wonderful music one can perhaps detect the influence of the muse who would attend Monk to the end of his life and did much to help turn his life around. This was Baroness Pannonica de Koenigswarter. Pannonica de Koenigswarter was born into the English line of the Rothschild family and grew up in Paris, attending a strict religious boarding school. Her lineage and education discouraged her from the traditional role of housewife. She learned to fly, and married a fellow pilot, the French diplomat and later resistance fighter Jules de Koenigswarter. In World War II she went on various missions for De Gaulle. Her brother served as Churchill's courier to the White House, and used the opportunity to take piano lessons with Teddy Wilson. Pannonica soon came to share her brother's enthusiasm for jazz.

When her husband served in the French embassy in Mexico City, this dynamic, emancipated woman grew bored with her life there. In 1951, at the age of thirty-seven, she came to New York and established herself at the best address, renting a luxury suite in the Stanhope Hotel on Fifth Avenue. The suite soon became a private meeting place for the predominantly black musicians of the modern style. It functioned as a kind of unconventional counterpart to the literary salons of eighteenth-century Europe.

In May 1954 the Baroness (called 'Nica' for short by musicians) flew to Paris and arrived just in time to attend the June 1 concert at which Monk appeared. She had wanted to introduce herself to Monk for some time. She recounts their first meeting in the film by Charlotte Zwerin thus: 'I didn't meet Monk until '54,' she says in aristocratic British English. 'I took the plane to Paris, just in time to see his first overseas concert. I went backstage afterwards, and Mary Lou Williams introduced me to him. And the rest of the time he was there we had a ball. Then I came back to

Monk and Baroness Nica de Koenigswarter

New York a couple of months later. I was then living in the Stanhope, but after Bird died [in her apartment, March 12, 1955] they threw me out, so I went to the Bolivar. And that's when I got my piano. And Thelonious and I got together. That's when he wrote 'Brilliant Corners' and 'Ba-Lue Bolivar Ba-lues-are.' At night we'd go out round to the clubs, and all the musicians would come back with us to the Bolivar and we'd have these fantastic jam sessions till eight or nine in the morning. So, of course, eventually that caused trouble, and I was thrown out of there. And then we decided that I should get a house of my own, and I got this house [overlooking the Hudson in Weehawken N.J., around 1971].'

It is important to note that Monk's relations with the Baroness do not seem to have affected the deep mutual understanding that he enjoyed with Nellie. The trio of Monk, Monk's mother, and Nellie seems now to have evolved into the constellation Monk, Nellie, and Nica. In any case Monk met this uniquely generous woman and patroness at a time when he and his family stood in especial need of material help and support.

This support, together with the artistic self-consciousness awakened in him by his warm reception in Europe and the success of the *Bags' Groove* recordings, may have made Monk all the more angry that Prestige had done so little for him, especially about getting his work permit back. On top of this, there was a dispute over the repayment of a trifling advance. The growth of his family with the birth of his daughter 'Boo Boo' taxed his financial condition to the limit, making his quarrel with Prestige over money that much more tiresome.

The Riverside Years
Breakthrough

THE DEATH OF CHARLIE PARKER IN MARCH OF 1955 MARKED CLEARLY and decisively the end of an era. The age of classic bebop was over. In his biography of Parker, Ross Russell describes how shifts in public taste bring new styles to the forefront of a culture every five years. These are the years in which a new generation reaches maturity, looking for new heroes. The attitude of the fan now was no longer typified by a cult of genius centered on an extravagantly large-living, self-destructive artist. It was more admiration for someone detached and self-possessed, master of both himself and his environment. Miles Davis, after kicking his heroin addiction (which was a relic of the Parker ethos), became the new star of modern jazz. No more were emotions flaunted with tearing, giddy, virtuosic lines. Now, instead, a minimum of emotion was conveyed through coolly restrained tones in a moderate tempo.

The Miles Davis' all-star recordings on *Bags' Groove* are an ideal example of the type. They illustrate another new trend in that Milt Jackson's playing, although it is virtuosic in the classic sense, demonstrates the earthy, arresting influence of gospel and the blues. This trend typifies Hard Bop and Soul Jazz, which were gaining popularity. The blending of gospel and blues with jazz introduced a quality described at the time as 'funky.' A year later Miles Davis, in his first classic quintet, would integrate his earlier cool manner with the new vigorous style, to form a trend-setting synthesis. Horace Silver and Art Blakey were protagonists of the new style and achieved immediate success with it. The greatest success, however, was reserved for Davis himself, who imposed a surface of 'cool' over a hard bopping rhythm section. Monk's piano playing could also be perceived as cool, intellectual, and funky, all at the same time. It remained oriented toward the melody, and therefore easy to follow. In this respect, again, he was an anomaly in bebop.

Since the Minton's days Monk had been an imposing figure. His size, over six feet tall and close to two hundred pounds, alone won him respect. And he was not governed by a self-destructive inner demon, like Powell or Parker. He simply filled the needs of his inner rhythm with self-discipline. His uncompromising individualism more and more fit the new public expectation of what a jazz star should be like. The parallel with Miles Davis in this respect is inevitable. It is significant that Davis' famous comeback at the Newport Festival in 1955 began with a standing ovation after a solo with muted trumpet on Monk's "Round Midnight.' Monk, moreover, was presiding at the piano in this performance of the all-star group.

At the beginning of 1955, however, this development was not yet clear. At Prestige they only knew that sales of Monk's records were poor. And so Bob Weinstock was not opposed to letting Monk out of his contract, pending settlement of the still outstanding dispute over money. The critic Nat Hentoff reported this fact to the people at Riverside.

Riverside was a small label, just recently founded. Billy Grauer and Orrin Keepnews had worked together since the end of the forties on the nonprofit jazz periodical *The Record Changer*. Now they brought Riverside into existence, and soon, by preference, made it their chief concern. Keepnews had been an inveterate fan of older, more traditional jazz, until he heard Thelonious Monk in 1948. In his enthusiasm he wrote one of the first feature articles about him. He wasted little time in loaning Monk the necessary $108.27 to erase his debt with Prestige. Riverside had their first star, and a basis for their existence.

Billy Grauer and Orrin Keepnews for a long time had wanted to work with an artist to whom they could give the opportunity to present his art in different contexts. At Riverside they tried to get away from the jam-session style 'blowing sessions' which were the regular practice at Prestige and which made artistically more ambitious projects difficult. In July Monk entered the studio for the first time with Riverside, accompanied by Kenny Clarke and bassist Oscar Pettiford. Together they had agreed to record an LP of Duke Ellington standards. Their evident intention was to erase the prejudice that Monk could only play his own compositions. This plan, and the limited success of the album, show that even the parties involved had not yet realized how much potential Monk's own music had with the public, and how much it had already grown.

An indication of this coming success is the fact that the shrewd jazz manager George Wein hired Monk for an all-star band with Miles Davis, the Cool Jazz saxophonists Zoot Sims and Gerry Mulligan, bassist Percy Heath, and the new drummer in the Modern Jazz Quartet, Connie Kay. They appeared that summer at the Newport Jazz Festival. Another record company, Signal, engaged Monk as a sideman for a recording that October, in a quartet led by alto saxophonist Gigi Gryce.

Shortly after the Signal recordings, the jazz enthusiast Harry Colomby (who made his living teaching English and history) met Monk in a New York nightclub. Art Blakey and his Jazz Messengers were performing. Colomby was there to discuss details with Blakey concerning a guest performance at Far Rockaway High School, where Colomby taught. Monk was simply there to see his

With Shadow Wilson and Oscar Pettiford
in concert, 1956

old friend. Colomby's brother Jules had been the producer on
the Signal recording session. Colomby used this as an opportunity to introduce himself to Monk. Monk asked him if he would
be willing to drive him home after the performance. The pianist
was struck by the other man's high estimate of him and his music.
Colomby for his part was impressed by the reserved, yet powerful dignity Monk radiated. When Monk asked whether he would
be willing to be his personal manager, Colomby promptly agreed.

Two years before his fortieth birthday Monk finally had the combination of conditions that were indispensable for a willful, artistic nature like his own to achieve commercial success: an intact family structure, a contract with an established and artistically ambitious record company, an able and devoted manager, and, in Nica de Koenigswarter, a generous friend and patroness, influential in the business world. The turn toward a breakthrough lay within his reach. Advance notice of this was given in December 1955 when Monk appeared on TV's Tonight Show with Steve Allen. He was in a sextet consisting of trumpet, tenor sax, trombone, piano, bass, and drums. A private tape (technically wretched) exists. Allen desperately tries to engage Monk in small talk. Monk does make an effort, but his embarrassment is painfully obvious, and he simply has no patience for TV talk. He responds to Allen's questions in sullen monosyllables.

But Monk and Riverside's recording programme had just begun. They followed the road once taken with their second album. Again with Oscar Pettiford on bass, and now with Monk's favorite drummer, Art Blakey (Kenny Clarke had since departed for Paris), Monk made a recording of classic jazz standards in March and April of 1956. The resulting album, *The Unique Thelonious Monk*, enjoyed considerable success. It ironically served to interest the public in the pianist's own compositions, since he was clearly capable of bringing such new and startling interpretations to other people's material.

In December of that same year Monk got the opportunity to record his own new compositions in a quintet. Sonny Rollins was on hand, as were Oscar Pettiford, and the man whom Kenny Clarke always referred to as the most intelligent drummer, Max Roach. Clark Terry plays trumpet on 'Bemsha Swing', the Monk original already recorded with Prestige. Ernie Henry on alto saxophone is the second horn, after Rollins, on the remaining num-

Art Blakey

bers. The title piece, 'Brilliant Corners', had such odd variations in rhythm that a version fit for release had to be created by the producer's patient editing, after many vain attempts to record a continuous take: so the producer himself, Orrin Keepnews, reports. Max Roach, recalling the date in a December 1996 interview, gives a rather different account. He says that Monk had tried for four days to get the musicians to learn the number by ear. 'The sidemen were only paid the minimum union tariff based on a six-hour day. When finally the producer got tired of our messing up the tune, Monk took out the music and handed it out to us, and we managed to play that difficult tune without problems. Monk had had the music ready to hand out at any moment for five days. He just wanted us to be paid as long as possible.' In any case, 'Brilliant Corners" fresh, vibrant quality struck even Monk insiders. It was the piece that helped the album achieve an unqualified success.

At the beginning of 1957, the efforts of Nica de Koenigswarter and Harry Colomby to bring Monk back into possession of a cabaret card finally paid off. With the help of expert medical opinion they were able to prove that Monk was no junkie. He had a car accident in his '56 Buick (which he remained faithful to for years to come). But after he recuperated he was able for the first time in years to secure a club engagement.

While the recovery of his cabaret card was pending, Monk was witness at Café Bohemia to a nearly physical altercation between Miles Davis and John Coltrane. Davis made clear to the saxophonist that he would no longer put up with his drug dependence and consequent unreliability. Monk went up to Coltrane afterward and told him that he didn't have to put up with that kind of abuse. He then mentioned the possibility of working together. Coltrane went right back to Pittsburgh and rid himself of his addiction cold turkey. When he returned to New York, he sought out Monk's 'house seminars.' There he would have often met the bassist Wilbur Ware, and drummer Shadow Wilson, who had played with Count Basie and also with Monk on a few of his Blue Note records.

These four musicians—Monk, Coltrane, Ware, and Wilson—then performed together in the spring and summer of 1957, at the new, trendsetting jazz club The Five Spot, on New York's Lower East Side. They also recorded some fine tracks that can be heard on *Thelonious Monk with John Coltrane.* Monk's reputation had by

With John Coltrane and Shadow Wilson at the Five Spot, 1957

this time grown to the point where the club's managers, Joe and Iggy Termini, told him to choose a new piano for the club and they would pay for it. The contract, moreover, had no set time limit. Monk's appearance became a triumphant homecoming. His appearance lasted five months, the club was consistently packed, and the line of people hoping to get in often reached the next block.

Monk had one cause for regret. The managers refused to allow him to bring a sextet or a quintet into the club, almost certainly for financial reasons. Their ostensible pretext was that the stage was too small. And so the classic Monk quartet had its origin in the arbitrary decision of a club owner.

During his collaboration with Monk, Coltrane's personal style first began to assert itself. 'My time with Monk brought me into association with a supreme architect of music,' Coltrane later said. 'I learned from him in every respect.' Coltrane at this time was under contract with Prestige. Monk refused to make any arrange-

John Coltrane

ment with his former company. Consequently the quartet was never recorded live. However, Coltrane's wife Naima made a private tape of the performance of September 11, when Coltrane was no longer a regular member of the quartet but was sitting in for the absent Johnny Griffin (who had since taken his place).

Also in 1957, the twenty-nine year old pianist Hampton Hawes surfaced in New York. He grew up in Los Angeles. During his California stint in 1945-46, Charlie Parker had become a personal and musical model for the young musicians there. Since then Hawes had attained to his own style in the Parker/Powell tradition. To jazz insiders he represented one of the most interesting musicians of his generation. But during this period in New York he was at the low point of his addiction to drugs.

In a club after a performance Hawes wanted to try out the electric keyboard that belonged to the bassist Slam Stewart. Stewart was not crazy about the idea: 'I never once let Art Tatum play it, and Tatum is the greatest pianist in the world!' he yelled. At which Hawes heard someone behind him bellow, 'Tatum isn't the greatest, and when you want to play on the thing, just do it!' Amazed, he turned and saw a giant towering over him, blacker than any African-American he had ever seen. On his nose were sunglasses with bamboo rims, in his hand was a bamboo cane. He looked like Jomo Kenyatta. This was the guise in which Monk was introduced to Hawes. With him was Nica de Koenigswarter, to whom Hawes was introduced later in the evening. From her he received the magical phone number that one had only to call to be spirited directly to her apartment by private limousine.

Monk looked after the young musician and became a father to him, as Hawes attests. When he first visited the Baroness, he found Monk lying on a brass bed, under a mink coverlet, wearing dirty shoes, and snoring loudly. The Baroness said to him, 'Shhh, Thelonious is sleeping'—as if they were in the room with a napping child. Despite Monk's solicitude, Hawes' condition would deteriorate. Monk and Nica repeatedly picked him up at night from a bench in Central Park. They usually took him to Monk's place, where he would be placed in the tub, then provided with fresh clothes.

In no case would Monk allow his protégé to feel despised because of his addiction. He, and occasionally his regular visitor Sonny Rollins who had had similar problems in the past, would remind him of his responsibility as an artist and role-model. In this way they helped him preserve a remnant of self-respect. When Hawes ran into his mentor years later in Los Angeles, Monk appeared not to want to recognize him, and ignored him for several minutes. But then Monk suddenly executed in front of him one of those lively dance steps which he would use to direct his band, and yelled, 'Hey, man, your sunglasses are still sitting in my apartment in New York.' Hawes discovered with pleasure that someone had been thinking about him all those years.

Hampton Hawes wondered whether Monk, this pivotal figure of the heroin-riddled bebop scene, did not take the drug himself. He came to this conclusion: 'If he took drugs, I didn't know about it. In any case it didn't show, and that, for me, is what it meant to be cool.'

Some aspects of the Monk legend that became entrenched during his long absence from public view were now belied, thanks to the efforts of Nica and Harry Colomby. Nica personally drove him to and from his appearances in her Bentley. For the most part the 'unreliable eccentric' showed up at work regularly and punctually. He was also more available for interviews. The reason for this, perhaps, is that Harry Colomby or Nellie were usually also on hand. It was not yet an easy matter to get him to sit for journalists, but Ira Gitler, Nat Hentoff, and Frank London Brown succeeded, and extracted some revealing statements from him:

'Everything that I play is different from others. The melody is different, the harmonies are different, the structure is different. Every piece is different. I may play a standard, for instance. When it begins to tell a story, when it gets a certain *sound*, then the thing clicks–the interpretation is perfect.'

'Do I believe that I am difficult to understand? Give me an example. Name me a specific number. Some of my pieces have melodies that any idiot could learn. I have written one that is in the same key from beginning to end. A tone-deaf person could hum it.'

'[For the album *Monk's Music*] Riverside asked that I allow myself to be photographed in a monk's habit, standing in a pulpit, holding a glass of whisky. I refused. For one thing, monks don't stand in pulpits. Then they wanted to put me in tie and tails. I said no to that too, and instead offered to seat myself in a little handwagon, because I had actually done some composing sitting in my son's little handwagon in the driveway.'

'I'll tell you, I have no time to think to consider what I should think about other musicians. I am too busy getting my own thing together.'

'When I was a kid some youths from the neighborhood tried to get me to hate the whites for everything that had been done to the blacks. And for a while I tried to do that. But every time I got to the point of hating them, a white person would come along who would put all my efforts back at the beginning.'

'My music makes no socially critical comment on race discrimination, poverty, or anything like that. I would have composed exactly the same even if I weren't black.' (It should be noted, however, that when asked later about this statement, Monk denied that he ever uttered it.)

Besides performing at the Five Spot, Monk in 1957 entered the studio five times for Riverside, each time with different com-

With Roy Haynes (d) and Johnny Griffin (ts) at the Five Spot in 1957

binations of instruments and personnel, including Coleman Hawkins and baritone saxophonist Gerry Mulligan. Monk's Riverside recordings are generally accounted among his best. The septet to which Hawkins contributed made the first recording of 'Crepuscule with Nellie.' This is a piece Monk wrote for his wife when she lay in the hospital seriously ill. He worked on it an entire month. When performing it in ensemble he never permitted solos, on the grounds that it would disrupt the dominant mood.

The powerful media concern CBS also began to take note of Monk's artistic and commercial success. In December 1957 they invited him to appear on their famous television show 'The Sound of Jazz.' A tape of the program is available (see list of videos at the end of the book). This particular program included jazz greats Count Basie, Coleman Hawkins, Billie Holiday, and Lester Young. Modern jazz was represented by Monk's trio and the Jimmy Giuffre Three. During Monk's spot Count Basie can be seen sitting on a bar stool in the bay of the piano, listening to his colleague with as much evident wonder as amusement. A smile of pride in his protégé is discernible on the lips of Coleman Hawkins, standing a little further off. Legend has it that Monk was so excited during the days before his appearance that he had trouble sleeping. An LP was to be marketed along with the show, and a recording date was set some days prior. When it arrived, Monk finally fell asleep and missed the date. That is the reason given for why Mal Waldron represents the modern, Monk school of piano on the record. Waldron insists that the recording session took place after the production of the show. He confirms the rest of the story, though: On the scheduled date there was no getting hold of Monk, and so Waldron finally made his first solo piano recording, in Monk's place. Understandably, he was a little nervous, and his number is consequently entitled 'Nervous.'

With Sonny Rollins, also at the Five Spot in 1957

In the quartet at the Five Spot John Coltrane was replaced by Johnny Griffin, whom Monk had met in 1955 in Chicago, and with whom he had made recordings in 1957 with Art Blakey's Jazz Messengers. Coltrane returned to the Miles Davis quintet a more self-aware and well-regarded musician. Later in the year Griffin's place was taken by Charlie Rouse, who would remain with Monk for ten years. His playing was more reserved and nonchalant than that of his predecessors.

On September 11, 1958, Monk and Charlie Rouse drove with the Baroness to Baltimore for a date. In Delaware they stopped before a hotel. Monk was thirsty and asked the manager at reception for a glass of water. The manager reacted hostilely, whereat Monk fell into a gloomy silence and began to pace the lobby. The manager found this giant stalking his hotel alarming, and called the police. When they arrived, Monk was already sitting in his car. They ordered him out, but Monk just stared straight ahead and didn't move. He was forced out of the car and handcuffed. The car was then thoroughly searched. In the Baroness' luggage they found some marijuana, which she declared to be hers. A charge against her would later be thrown out. Monk, however, would be found guilty of trespassing. For the New York police it was grounds once again for depriving him of his cabaret card, this time for two years. Harry Colomby protested that the hotel manager had engaged in racist behavior. But because Monk wouldn't confirm that the manager had called him 'nigger', his appeal was denied.

As when he lost his cabaret card the first time, Monk had few opportunities to appear publicly in New York, and he was reluctant to play elsewhere. An episode in the autumn of 1959 did not help. It incidentally shows how, while his professional career was thriving, his psychological problems were getting worse. He was booked in Boston, and arrived at his hotel very late. He proceeded

With pianist Horace Silver during the *Sonny Rollins Volume 2*
session, Hackensack New Jersey, 1957

to take a few turns in the lobby, staring at the walls. The hotel manager, when Monk finally asked him for his room, took him for a nut and refused to give it to him. Monk went to his engagement, played two numbers with his band, then called for a break. Around 11:30 he returned to the stage, and played the same numbers again. He then sat for some time before the piano in silence. At this point the band packed up and left. Finally Monk himself departed. He took a taxi to the airport in hopes of catching a flight to New York. But the flights had all left. He roamed the airport grounds in silence, until state police picked him up and took him to Grafton State Hospital in Worcester. He was held there a week for psychiatric observation. At his home, meanwhile, no one knew where he was. The Boston police could give no information, and no one thought to ask the state police. A telegram from the hospital was never received.

From then on, Monk rarely travelled alone. Usually Nellie accompanied him. When necessary, Harry Colomby or Colomby's brother would fill in as his escort. Monk would regularly deflect questions as to his eccentricity with the remark, 'I can't be crazy. They had me in a nut house once and let me go.'

Again as when he first lost his cabaret card, Thelonious and Nellie shielded the children from knowledge of his problems. Monk used his enforced free time, as his son would later report, to play piano from morning to night. To his family he was anything but the silent, mysterious man he was perceived to be in public. In a 1993 interview, Nellie described him thus: 'Thelonious had continuous nonsense in his head: joking, teasing, napping. We had so much fun.' Thelonious Jr. agrees with her: 'Thelonious was a true family guy. He was always in the mood for fun and loved to play with us kids. Card games, dice games, jazzy games, poker games.'

In spite of losing his cabaret card, Monk no longer had to

contend for recognition. His albums were universally praised. His appearances were handled by Joe Glaser's powerful Associated Booking Association. The fee for the quartet for a single evening was $800 two years earlier, now it was $1,000. He was an overwhelming favorite at the Newport Festival. In July 1959 he recorded some numbers for Roger Vadim's film 'Les Liaisons Dangereuses.' Now was also the time to take advantage of the interest in Monk in the rest of the world, particularly in the expanding European market. The quartet toured Europe annually from 1960 to 1967. They also made appearances in jazz-hungry Japan.

For some time Monk had been working with the 'third-stream' composer Hall Overton. Overton was taken with Monk's compositions, and in collaboration with the pianist arranged them for a large band. In February 1959, the arrangements were performed with a ten-piece orchestra in New York's Town Hall. At Riverside they had the foresight to record the event. The public and the majority of critics were enthusiastic about the resulting album, *The Thelonious Monk Orchestra at Town Hall.* In autumn of the same year Monk traveled to appearances in California. A concert at the Hollywood Bowl struck many observers as chaotic. It appeared to revive the rumors of Monk's undependability. He started out playing an uncertain 'Misterioso' with the quartet, accompanying Charlie Rouse with elbow clusters. There followed a heated discussion about what to play next. Monk cut it short by playing the opening notes of ''Round Midnight.' After this number he abruptly left the stage and did not return.

The owner of the Blackhawk club in San Francisco had never hired Monk up to this point because of this very behavior. Nevertheless, he now wanted to share in the Monk boom, and, before the Hollywood Bowl fiasco he had already engaged him with a band of prominent local musicians. Naturally, he was anxious about whether things would go smoothly. On the first evening

A poster from the quartet's European tour in 1961

Monk was the only musician to show up on time. Everything went well thereafter, and the engagement, which lasted several weeks, was a critical triumph that also drew large audiences.

During his time in San Francisco Monk recorded his second American solo album. Up to this point Riverside had undertaken to produce albums that consistently presented Monk in new settings, and, as far as possible, with at least a few new numbers. In his live appearances with the quartet, however, Monk confined himself for the most part to titles from the Blue Note and Prestige years. The pieces were also performed in a rather inflexible format: theme, saxophone solo, piano solo, (usually) a bass and drum solo, then recapitulation of the theme. The disciplined saxophone style of Charlie Rouse, which translated Monk's ideas perfectly into continuous lines, does not have the same attraction for the average listener as the style of a Sonny Rollins or Johnny Griffin. Monk's piano style, on the other hand, strikes most listeners as charmingly unique. But in the ritualized quartet context its cryptic, laconic quality can be difficult to decipher, and soon becomes monotonous. The excitement of a live performance could help offset this reaction, but the potential for monotony still had to be reckoned with when planning an album.

Riverside was aware of this. In April of 1960 they first recorded the quartet live with the usual personnel, including Charlie Rouse. The same month Monk was also recorded at the Blackhawk, only this time the trumpeter Joe Gordon and saxophonist Harold Land, both of whom lived on the West Coast, were added for the sake of variety.

In February 1961 the Monks' apartment was the victim of fire. Fortunately the Steinway escaped undamaged.

In light of Monk's international success, the media company CBS, already doing good business with Miles Davis and Dave Brubeck, made him an offer. For all his eccentricity Monk was a shrewd businessman and never sold himself short. He saw his

Charlie Rouse

chance and decided to make the move to this international concern (whose records were issued under the Columbia imprint).

At Riverside they were naturally not pleased that the artist
whom they had brought along for years was now taking the fruits
of their labor elsewhere. But anyone who knows the volatile jazz
business knows that one must capitalize on one's chances. Orrin
Keepnews and Billy Grauer were reluctant to let the pianist go
before he had fulfilled his contractual obligations. They asserted
their claims in a brief to the musicians' labor union. The union
affirmed the rights of the small label. Yet how was one to induce a
musician to do creative work when he no longer wished to work
for you at all?

At this point luck came to Riverside's aid. In Europe, as well
as Japan, the concerts were often co-produced by radio stations
that secured to themselves the recording priveleges. Billy Grauer
managed to obtain the rights for the concerts from the Olympia
in Paris and the Teatro Lirico in Milan. With these recordings
Riverside had enough material for the albums Monk still owed
them, and thus an elegant solution was found agreeable to all
parties. Monk's obligations to Riverside actually ended with the
first live recording they released, consisting of the regular quartet
with Charlie Rouse. That they were produced by a company other
than Riverside lends a symbolic note to the ending.

The Columbia Years
International Stardom

ON OCTOBER 31, 1962 MONK'S QUARTET ENTERED THE CBS STUDIOS
for the first time. The group had played together for over a year;
besides Charlie Rouse, it consisted of John Ore on bass and Frankie
Dunlop on drums. In February 1963 Monk was back in the studio
with the same lineup. In May the quartet, now with Butch Warren on bass, were guest stars in Tokyo, where the concert was
taped for general release. In July the quartet again appeared at

The Thelonious Monk Quartet, with John Ore (b),
Frankie Dunlop (d), and Charlie Rouse (ts)

An example of Monk's eccentric taste in headgear. He not only performed
with this Chinese hat, but liked to play basketball in it.

the Newport Jazz Festival, and again CBS captured the event on
record. In September the quartet played two days at the Monterey
Jazz Festival.

That same month, the Five Spot, which had moved into larger
quarters a few blocks away from its original location, celebrated
its new address with a guest appearance by the Thelonious Monk
Quartet. This time they remained six months. Leroi Jones (Amiri
Baraka), the poet and critic, in his book *Black Music* describes the
nightly ritual of Monk's band. Monk would show up around
eleven, go to the dressing room to prepare himself, order a double
bourbon at the bar, then, drink in hand, would mount the stage.
Here he would play an unaccompanied piano solo. Then he would

approach the microphone. 'Now Frankie Dunlop will play you some tubs', he would say, and disappear behind the stage. After the drum solo he would return, again approach the microphone, and say: 'Butch Warren will play a bass solo.' And again he would vanish during the bass solo. The entire quartet might play its first set this way. The pieces they played were drawn from the established repertoire of Monk tunes. One or another piece would sometimes be played twice the same evening in different sets. The ensemble playing of the quartet is so precise and elegant, that Leroi Jones sometimes found himself wishing that Charlie Rouse's playing would be less refined, and instead more earthy and emotionally arresting.

While the other musicians performed their solos, Monk often executed dance steps before the piano, directing the group with his body language. These trancelike steps were Monk's way of telling the band that he approved of their playing. Newcomers to Monk often assume that they were done for the sake of effect. Band members, however, insist that these dances were no publicity stunt, but an entirely natural thing. Monk's outward appearance could also, mistakenly, appear to aim at deliberate mystification. Now he always appeared with some new, exotic headgear. Below the neck, however, his clothing always bespoke a very conventional elegance.

In large part owing to CBS's marketing strategy, Monk was now known outside the world of jazz. *Time* magazine planned a cover story on him for November 1963. It had to be delayed, however, after the Kennedy assassination.

Another event was even more gratifying for Monk than the feature planned for *Time.* Right in the neighborhood where he had long ago settled with his mother and still resided, Lincoln Center with Philharmonic Hall had been built, restoring the value of the whole area. On December 30, 1963 Monk gave a concert in Philharmonic Hall with his quartet and a big band assembled

and rehearsed by Hall Overton. The public and critics were ec-
static. This concert was recorded by CBS.

The cover story in *Time* finally appeared in February 1964. It
is soundly researched and very thorough. This wave of success
and notoriety seemed to make Monk once more friendly to journalists, so long as they evinced a genuine interest in his music.
Thus between 1963 and 1965 he gave a series of interviews with
some very revealing statements:

'Those who want to know what sound goes into my music,
should come to New York and open their ears.'

'I say, play your own way. Don't play what the public wants.
You play what you want and let the public pick up on what you're
doing–even if it does take them fifteen, twenty years.'

'I never listen to Ellington. If there are similarities in our playing, it must be a coincidence. Recently I sat in on piano with his
orchestra on a couple of numbers. [This was at Newport, July 8,
1962.] That was quite an interesting experience for me, but nothing more. Duke actually played very little piano with his orchestra. I tell you again, I stopped listening to him years ago, so he
cannot possibly have influenced me. If there is influence, maybe
it goes in the opposite direction.'

'I don't consider myself a musician who has achieved perfec-
tion and can't develop any further. But I compose my pieces with
a formula that I created myself. Take a musician like John Coltrane. He is a perfect musician, who can give expression to all the
possibilities of his instrument. But he seems to have difficulty expressing original ideas on it. That is why he keeps looking for
ideas in exotic places. At least I don't have that problem, because,
like I say, I find my inspiration in myself.'

'At this time the fashion is to bring something to jazz that I
reject. They speak of freedom. But one has no right, under pretext of freeing yourself, to be illogical and incoherent by getting
rid of structure and simply piling a lot of notes one on top of the

Monk on the cover of *Time* magazine, February 28, 1964

other. There's no beat anymore. You can't keep time with your foot. I believe that what is happening to jazz with people like Ornette Coleman, for instance, is bad. There's a new idea that consists in destroying everything and finding what's shocking and unexpected; whereas jazz must first of all tell a story that anyone can understand.'

'I don't read newspapers and I don't read books. I keep abreast of things by watching TV.'

'I like to sleep. There is no set time of day for sleep. You sleep when you're tired, that's all there is to it.'

'I don't worry about the color of my skin. I never think about the fact that I'm black. Or rather, I would rather not think about it. I have no desire to imagine to myself what would be different in my life if I had a different skin color.'

'I know nothing about racial divisions. I never took any interest in these Muslims. If you want to know something about them, ask Art Blakey. I never had to change my name, it was weird enough already. I also haven't written any of these 'Freedom Suites', and I have no plans to.'

Nellie Monk was widely quoted in the press as well:

'The whole time he thinks about nothing but music, even if he doesn't talk about it directly. He can stand in the middle of a room full of people, and compose. I don't know anyone else so capable of withdrawing into himself.'

'We live music every day. Thelonious never looked to do anything else but make music. He was, and is, an optimist.'

The optimist would nevertheless sometimes shut himself off from his environment completely, take to his bed, and go for days with speaking. No one knew in those cases what was going on inside him. His psychotic episodes sometimes occurred even during performance. The pop musician Captain Beefheart experienced it firsthand at a concert in the San Fernando Valley. 'They gave him a grand piano, a really beautiful Steinway, surmounted by a cut-glass bowl full of roses. He came in late wearing a trench coat. He dumped the bowl in the piano, knocked down the lid, and hit one note. The sound: everything going into the piano, the strings, the water splashing, the roses. Then he left.' Captain Beefheart characterizes this as 'the most memorable performance I ever witnessed.' In fact, these crazy incidents had become part of the Monk trademark. He was plainly aware of the impression they created. In the film *Straight, No Chaser* he can be seen turning pirouettes in the kitchen of the Village Vanguard, and saying to the camera, 'I do that out in the street sometimes. Somebody else doing that, they'd put him in a straight jacket.' And after a pause, with which he seems to suggest that it was expected of him, he adds, 'Oh, it's only Thelonious Monk. He's crazy!'

After turning circles Monk might freeze altogether, fixing bewildered observers with a stare. Slowly the rigid stare would soften to his usual, distinctive look, which has often been described as having a mysterious power. Its effect derived in part from a slight squint, and the peculiar expression of Monk's mouth, enhanced by the often crosswise position of his jaws. This look would then dissolve into a happy beam that made the whole face radiate with the innocence of a child.

In 1964 Ben Riley replaced Frankie Dunlop on drums, and Larry Gales replaced Butch Warren on bass. This new group could be heard until 1968 at the large jazz festivals in the US, Europe, and to a lesser extent, Japan. CBS recorded the quartet regularly through 1967, though at ever wider intervals. On his European tours Monk, who was shy of human contact, sometimes had American musicians who had transplanted to Europe work for him as road managers. One recounts with amusement that at the hotels Thelonious and Nellie were constantly preoccupied with packing and unpacking their suitcases. Like a good housewife Nellie also looked after the money. She could be seen carefully counting bills over and over. On his tour of Australia in 1965, also, she was very much the cost-conscious housewife, as could be seen from the size of their baggage. One box was full of Coca-Cola bottles that had to be returned for deposits. They also traveled with an iron and ironing board. Monk's luggage was swelled with fourteen suits and seventeen pairs of shoes. In the land of the kangaroo no one, at least, would mistake him for a tramp. On these trips abroad he also had the opportunity to purchase various different kinds of headwear. A black silk skullcap that he picked up in Hong Kong became his favorite.

In 1966 Monk took his first and only 'blindfold test.' This was a special type of interview conducted by Leonard Feather, designed for musicians to give unbiased, critical reactions to other musicians. Feather invited them to his house and played them recordings, without telling them anything about the music they were about to hear. The results of this test appeared almost monthly in the pages of *Down Beat,* and the feature enjoyed great popularity. Monk's blindfold test appeared in April 1966. Monk did not seem very interested in listening to other musicians unless they were playing one of his own compositions. With the interpretation of his own tunes he noted every departure from the original. He reacted to the Oscar Peterson trio's playing of 'Easy Listenin' Blues' by asking the way to the bathroom. He waited until the end of the record, though, before leaving. On returning he laughed and remarked, 'Well, you see where I went.' Asked his opinion of the guitarist on the track (Herb Ellis), he replied, 'Charlie Christian spoiled me for everybody else.' Only Denny Zeitlin, the psychoanalyst and pianist, was able to excite him with his playing of Monk's composition 'Carole's Garden.'

In 1967 Monk visited Europe with a nine-piece band. It was

the quartet, augmented by trumpeters Ray Copeland and Clark Terry, trombonist Jimmy Cleveland, alto saxophonist Phil Woods, and Johnny Griffin on tenor. The group was not particularly well rehearsed–they did not get the music until they were on the plane–but they were already conversant with and generally devoted to Monk's art. Critics and public alike were enthusiastic, and thankful for the change from the quartet concerts of previous years.

For this reason it is hard to understand why CBS did not take the opportunity to produce a studio album with such a talented group, and one so cut to Monk's mold–especially as the quartet recordings were now receiving only polite notices in the press. A French critic entitled his review of a Monk concert 'Monk in the hour of the Phantom.' He criticized him for ritualizing the facade of a once exciting music. In this respect Monk was only doing what he had done all these years: remaining inalterably true to himself. Asked why he always played the same pieces, he would answer, 'In order to create an audience for them.'

In the fall of 1968 it became clear that CBS was also growing tired of the Monk quartet. They decided to record him in Hollywood with a studio big band. The leader was Oliver Nelson, one of the industry's top arrangers of film music. Nelson also wrote the arrangements, which turned out very slick and bombastic. They are the antithesis of Monk's aesthetic. This was the last record Monk would make for CBS.

To be sure, CBS still wanted to produce Monk, but on their own terms. They sent him a collection of Beatles compositions and asked him to run them by someone who could play the tunes for him–as if he were incapable of reading music himself. From a commercial standpoint, using Beatles material was certainly not ill-conceived. Before they became countercultural icons the Beatles were groomed by their management to find favor with an older audience, an effort formally recognized when they won The Order of the British Empire. CBS's business philosophy was based entirely on this sort of arrant calculation. It had already led to Monk's music being debased and massacred by Oliver Nelson. Naturally, little more could be expected between him and CBS. In fact, the expiration of this, his last record contract, marks the beginning of Monk's gradual lapse into silence.

'The Purpose of Life'

IN 1969 LARRY GALES AND BEN RILEY LEFT THE QUARTET AND MONK
had trouble finding long-term replacements. Although he was able
to maintain a first-rate band with temporary players, he was increasingly worn down by personnel problems. As a result, he and
Charlie Rouse, the nucleus of the quartet, sometimes performed
as a duo.

Certainly the music scene had changed drastically in the preceding ten years. Free jazz was the rage. It functioned as a musical
pendant to the contemporary protest movement, especially in Europe. Yet Monk still regularly appeared, as he had for years, at the
Village Vanguard or Village Gate. He was also a frequent guest at
Club Baron, in Harlem. In the fall of 1969 he visited Europe with
the quartet, and made a memorable solo appearance at the Berlin
Jazz Festival. The organizer, Joachim Ernst Berendt, had intended
this as a tribute to Duke Ellington on his seventieth birthday. Monk
was prepared in his solo outing to play pieces by Ellington exclusively. He worked the piano as if he were in a trance. He grunted,
stamped his feet, and made his left hand jump powerfully all over.
The energy grew from piece to piece. The audience in this capital
of the protest movement, mainly receptive to free jazz, were ec-
static. When it came time for an encore, Monk played one of his
own pieces. He did so with a concentrated intensity, as if the performance up to that point had been only a prelude. Now he was
going to show them what he was really about. Inspired by the

applause, he then played extremely cooperatively with the stride pianist Joe Turner, accompanied by bass and drums. TV cameras were on hand, and show everything in close-up. After his appearance Monk sat down quietly next to Nellie in the vestibule behind the stage, looking old and tired.

After Berlin he toured the rest of Europe with the quartet. In December he played Paris. There Monk was so upset by the inept playing of his teenage drummer Austin Wright that after the break he brought Philly Joe Jones, who was resting backstage, up on the podium. All this was captured on television.

At the beginning of 1970, Charlie Rouse, sick of the continual changes in the rhythm section, left the quartet during an engagement at the Village Vanguard. He later had kind words for Monk both as a leader and a friend. He called him a master who knew how to bring the best out of his fellow musicians: Monk demanded almost the impossible from them, but inspired them with the confidence that they could produce it. With Rouse's departure, Monk no longer tended to the substitutions himself; Wilbur Ware, the bassist in the band, brought the baritone saxophonist Pat Patrick into the quartet.

Monk appeared to have lost his native optimism. At home, it is true, one could still find him in good humor. Patrick reports that in playful moods he would sometimes perform in the style of Fats Waller or Art Tatum. In that year, however, Monk did not tour Europe, although he did make a guest appearance in Japan, again with different personnel. Back from Japan, he next went to California with the tenor saxophonist Paul Jeffrey, who would remain Monk's regular horn player until the end. He played there six full months, with continually changing bassists and drummers. He was waiting until the situation in New York was settled. The tenants above his apartment wanted him evicted from his old home for making too much noise.

In April 1971 Monk returned to New York. He tried to put

together a quartet with Paul Jeffrey, and engaged his son Thelonious Jr. as drummer. They appeared at a jazz festival in Mexico, where he also gave his final interview. No trace of his dynamic optimism remains. To the interviewer, Pearl Gonzales', last question, 'What is the purpose of life?', Monk replies, 'To die.' To the interviewer's objection, that between life and death there was surely much to do, Monk countered: 'You asked me a question, that's the answer.'

This answer seems like a distant, tired echo of a conversation Monk had with the American drummer and onetime Monk sideman, Art Taylor, in Paris on October 15 the same year. Asked what his attitude to the black power movement was, Monk replied: 'I did all that fighting with ofays when I was a kid. We had to fight to make it so we could walk the streets. There's no reason why I should go through that black power shit now. I guess everybody in New York had to do that, right? Because every block is a different town. It was mean all over New York, all the boroughs. Then, besides fighting the ofays, you had to fight each other. You go in the next block and you're in another country. Don't look at a chick living in the next block and expect to be taking her home and all that; you might not make it. All people have got to do is make friends with each other.'

Taylor: 'Do the kids seem more aware now than they did years ago?'

Monk: 'I don't know. I was aware of all this when I was a little baby, five or six or seven years old. I was aware of how the cops used to act. It looked like the order of the day was for the cops to go out and call all the kids black bastards. Anything you did, if you ran or something, they called you black bastards.'

Taylor: 'That was their favorite lick.'

Monk: 'Yeah, I remember that; it was the first thing that came out of their mouth.'

Taylor: 'I consider myself lucky to have survived.'

Monk: 'Sure you're lucky to have survived, you're lucky to survive every second. You're facing death at all times. You don't know where it's going to come from.'

Monk was tired of the duties of being a band leader. It is therefore not surprising that he accepted the offer of George Wein to go on a world tour with an all-star group of bebop greats. After the financial success of 1971, these 'Giants of Jazz' went on tour again in 1972, including Europe. Dizzy Gillespie played trumpet, Kai Winding trombone, Sonny Stitt saxophone, Al McKibbon bass, and Art Blakey drums. Because all six musicians had once been bandleaders, and no one wanted, or was able, to dictate to the rest, they confined themselves to a repertoire of bebop standards. These are performed rather indifferently in a blowing-session manner. The financial motive took precedence over artistic considerations.

During the band's first European engagement in 1971, the British label Black Lion seized the initiative and asked Monk to make solo recordings, and trio recordings with Al McKibbon and Art Blakey. Monk agreed, and in a relaxed atmosphere, to which Nellie Monk's presence in the studio certainly contributed, three LPs were recorded. Blakey and McKibbon enjoyed being sidemen again for their former boss, the more so as they were of the opinion that Monk's music was not being performed properly by the other 'Giants of Jazz.' Thus the last recordings that Monk was to make as a bandleader were in London. They actually number among his best.

At the beginning of 1973 Monk was again at the Village Vanguard, then in February at Top of the Gate, the piano restaurant above the Village Gate. He had to interrupt this engagement owing to a lingering illness. And he made clear that he did not want to appear in clubs any longer. In general he was in decline; he was disposed to depression and suffered from memory lapses. Two years earlier he had been admitted to a New York hospital because of a slight stroke and lung inflammation. The Baroness says this about his sickness: 'This was the first year he lived here [in her newly acquired house in Weehawken, NJ]. We were driving home from New York, and he suddenly turned to me and said, "I am very seriously ill." This is the only thing Thelonious has ever been heard to say about being ill, at all. He never said it again.' Concerning Monk's unwillingness to appear publicly, Charlie Rouse says simply, 'Something really clicked in him. He didn't want to play anymore.'

In April 1974, Monk surfaced unexpectedly at a concert of the New York Jazz Repertory Company in Carnegie Hall dedicated to his compositions. His participation had been planned, but he had not shown up at rehearsals. Barry Harris was preparing to seat himself at the piano when Monk suddenly appeared on stage. (Barry Harris had come to New York, become a 'house seminarian', and was now Monk's closest friend, after Nica de Koenigswarter.)

The success of the concert may have induced Monk to participate in 'Newport in New York.' And so on July 3, 1975, a quartet consisting of him, Paul Jeffrey, Larry Ridley, and Thelonious Jr. played at Lincoln Center as part of this event. After a layoff of nearly a year, on March 26, 1976 he played with the same quartet plus guest trumpeter Lonnie Hillyer at Carnegie Hall. At Carnegie Hall again, on June 30 of the same year, and with the same quartet, he gave the last concert of his life. On July 4 he popped up at Bradley's, the New York piano bar where Barry Harris was performing. He sat in on piano for a pair of numbers. He then disappeared into the night and out of the jazz world altogether.

During his last years Monk withdrew to Nica de Koenigswarter's estate in New Jersey. He spent most of his time lying in bed watching television. Laurent de Wilde reports that during this period he had bladder and prostate operations. The quality of his life suffered as a result. From the outside world he

With Thelonious Jr. (d), Larry Ridley (b), and Paul Jeffrey (ts)
at Avery Fisher Hall in New York City, July 3, 1975

would admit only a few close friends and associates, like Barry Harris. Harris says: 'He was psychologically ill, no one could say for certain what was wrong with him. He simply resigned himself and did nothing. In his last years he generally did not play.' As a living corpse, whose spirit was tied to the atrophied shackles of his body, he simply existed.

On February 5, 1982 Thelonious Monk suffered a stroke, to which he succumbed on the 17th of February 1982, without ever again gaining consciousness. He died at Nica de Koenigswarter's estate, in the arms of his wife Nellie.

Monk during the *Genius of Modern Music Volume 2*
sessions, New York, May 1952

PART 2

MONK'S MUSIC

The Monk Sound

WHEN MONK ARRIVED ON THE NEW YORK JAZZ SCENE AROUND 1940, his personal style was already fully developed. Throughout his life, he was seriously interested in nothing besides his music, which from an early point on shows no stylistic break or alteration. His interpretations are always marked by a fresh, deeply probing exploration of the material. The material for the most part consists of compositions that Monk wrote during the second half of the forties, and first half of the fifties.

On every recording to which Monk is known to have contributed, he plays in his unmistakable style. In his biography Dizzy Gillespie states that he never heard Monk play differently. Oscar Pettiford confirms this, as does Kenny Clarke, whose acquaintance with Monk dates back to their school days. Clarke, to be sure, says that when Monk played gospel music in those days there was nothing distinctive about his playing. And Mary Lou Williams heard Monk when he was just out of school, at a jam session in Kansas City, where he made a stop in the late thirties accompanying a traveling evangelist. She ascribes to him at that time a fast, fluent style, one that was nevertheless different from swing. But it is safe to say that from the moment he emerged as a jazz pianist, he always played only as Monk.

The recordings that Jerry Newman made in 1941 at Minton's Playhouse with Charlie Christian, Joe Guy, and Kenny Clarke—and Monk, supposedly—appear to contradict this. But Henri

Renaud, who did a good deal of work with Monk, identified Kenny Kersey as the pianist on these recordings. Jacques Réda (*Jazz Magazine*, Paris, June 1979), compared these with the Jerry Newman recordings made with Don Byas the same year, to which Monk certainly did contribute, and in his inimitable style. He proved conclusively that Monk could not have been on hand for the much-discussed recording with Charlie Christian that reportedly shows his playing originally under the influence of Teddy Wilson. This agrees with the assertion of Laurent de Wilde that Monk and Christian never recorded together. Monk himself says that, from the beginning, he always expressed himself in the same idiom, and that no one else's ideas influenced him. Dizzy Gillespie says expressly and emphatically, that he never heard Monk play like Teddy Wilson—or anyone else, for that matter. He also identifies Ken Kersey as the pianist on the recordings with Charlie Christian.

'Whoever can't recognize Monk had better turn in his union card.' This is what Cal Tjader said during a blindfold test. In fact hardly any other pianist has as distinctive a sound. And 'sound' was the controlling word in Monk's discussions with fellow musicians. Monk was concerned above all with sound—sounds with which he might portray his beloved New York and the people that surrounded him there.

But as soon as the critic tries to describe what this sound is, he or she wanders off into realms of profound mystification. One reads of strangely tuned pianos such as those found on the early Prestige recordings. But during this period, Monk, from a commercial standpoint, was very much a gamble, and to his chagrin the record company skimped on piano tuners (as also later on the Five Spot recordings made by Mal Waldron, with Eric Dolphy and Booker Little).

There is, nevertheless, a peculiarly disharmonious harmony

to his music. First of all, there is the unconventional tone production, which is to say, his harshly percussive sound. Attention to touch as a factor in tone production in the western classical sense is rare in jazz circles. It is nonetheless standard practice to hold the hands with the fingers bent and spread–and this applies not only to the fast, brilliant playing of an Art Tatum, but also to the rapid blowing lines of a Bud Powell. But Thelonious Monk, this huge giant of a man with small, feminine hands, used a different technique entirely. Whiplike his hands would dart to the keys, and hammer them as a drummer strikes the skins with his sticks. This technique, essentially percussive in character, stands in contrast to a technique designed for speed and fluency. But to interpret this as a sign of pianistic ineptitude is to fail to appreciate Monk's peculiar kind of virtuosity.

It should be clear that anyone who grew up in the capital of America's musical life, and devoted himself to the piano for hours a day from earliest youth, does not play with a certain technique because of 'inability', but because he has consciously chosen it. When Monk wants to demonstrate fluency–as in his beloved whole-tone runs, or the diatonic, occasionally chromatic quadruplet and quintuplet figures–he does so masterfully.

In the area of tone production, too, belongs Monk's preference for the minor second. This has been differently interpreted as a pianistic approximation to quarter-tones, whereby the note lying between two semi-tones is implied (see the Musical Glossary in the back of the book, for these and other musical terms.) More careful observation reveals that the two notes of the interval are rarely played at equal volume. More often they are struck with different intensity, so that the more heavily accented one proper to the scale alone is sustained. This subtle blending of tones creates the impression that Monk is gliding from note to note, as when horn players produce 'blue notes' via bending of the note. (Milt Jackson would translate this keyboard-style technique of note-bending to the vibraphone.) Often these minor seconds are inserted as tonally veiled shorthand for a ninth chord.

This brings us to another characteristic of Monk's sound. Over long stretches his piano style is abrupt and markedly spare, as much vertical as horizontal. It is common for pauses to serve as contrasting elements of rhythm and sound. Then chords will unexpectedly appear that seem to destroy the tonality with their inclusion of notes foreign to the chord and even to the scale–all the better to affirm it, indirectly, in due course.

The almost unconscious control of the composition with its harmonic framework is the basis for this masterful effusion of sound. Dizzy Gillespie's statement was valid even in the days of Minton's Playhouse: 'If you want to play with Monk, you have to have the composition and the harmony down cold, otherwise you turn around and suddenly are faced with the greatest difficulties.' Ornette Coleman reproached the conventional players of changes by saying, 'I want to play the music, not the background.' That never applied to Monk, who, by contrast, worked with the whole structure of the piece in his solos, chords, initial rhythmic accents, and melody. All this went to realize his highly original idea of sound–'the music', in short.

On the basis of the vertical structure of a piece, Monk developed horizontal ideas that often have the character of brief, repeated variations on the piece's thematic and rhythmic material. With this approach, it is obvious that the manual division of labor standard in bebop, with the right hand playing single notes while the left hand sketches the underling harmony, no longer serves. Monk's sound, especially on the solo recordings, depends on giving both hands equal time. In this respect he can be said to belong to the tradition of the great Harlem stride pianists, even Art Tatum.

It is interesting that Monk, whenever someone criticized him for being unable to articulate his phrases clearly the way Art Tatum did, would reply ironically that he once played like Art Tatum, but found that it resulted in too many notes at once, and he was resolved to play only a few. The stride technique, also, was for him just one means among others of expressing sound—one, to be sure, that he revered. In any case, Monk's two-handed style of playing recalls Tatum and the stride pianists in that the left hand furnishes what in bebop is furnished by the rhythm section. The new role of the rhythm section led finally to the typical bebop development whereby the left hand at the piano only sporadically supplied the chord changes to the right hand, which in turn imitated the melodic line of a horn. Monk's right hand, in contrast, does not play blowing lines. It condenses pianistically what a horn player would articulate in long runs, while the left juxtaposes bass lines or elliptical chords. Ultimately, it all serves the needs of his characteristic sound.

Owing to his 'ambidextrous' style of playing, Thelonious Monk was destined to be the first modern pianist to make definitive solo recordings. In fact, on his first solo album, recorded in Paris in 1954, he does not play much differently than on his earlier, combo recordings. In these solo recordings, however, a further trait of the typical Monk sound emerges. The deeply probing horizontal developments draw a good part of their intensity from the rhythmic tension that results from the fact that in the coordination of the hands, often for whole measures at a time, neither one nor the other clearly marks time. In his later solo recordings Monk came increasingly to exploit the opportunities for rubato inherent in this style. But even then the rhythmic throb of his phrasing is so solid that the quality of the swing even in free, delayed beats, remains strong.

Alongside this rubato technique, Monk in his solo performances also reverted at appropriate moments to bass figures that help mark the beat. He derived these from stride, and used them especially when performing standards. What emerges thereby is

At the Rhode Island School of Design in October 1964.
Note the unorthodox style of attack.

no parody, but a humorous transposition of the older material into Monk's own musical world. This process of transposition is all the more notable in that Monk never wanders too far from the theme, so that the melody lines always remain in the hearer's consciousness as a contrasting foil. And yet many of Monk's solo recordings, especially the album *Solo Monk*, owing to the whole-sale importation of the stride technique, strike this reviewer as somewhat monotonous.

The Ensemble Pianist

THELONIOUS MONK'S PERSONAL STYLE DEVELOPED IN AN ENSEMBLE context: Minton's Playhouse at the beginning of the forties. The most important innovation of the Minton circle was in the area of rhythm. At the drums sat the man who with his brightly pulsing beat was responsible for the rhythmic conception of modern jazz, Kenny Clarke. He was at the same time the nominal leader. The generous Dizzy Gillespie—generous in his own contributions to jazz, as well as in his judgment of others—affirmed Kenny Clarke's importance in no uncertain terms.

The rhythmically contrapuntal accents in Clarke's playing have often been overrated for their significance in the development of jazz. The real significance of his approach lies in the liberating influence of his handling of the beat through his wonderfully sparkling use of the large cymbal. The beat is anchored there as securely as a metronome, and yet flows so smoothly—or better, pulses like a heartbeat—that the tempo emerges freely breathing. Clarke himself described to me the influence of this new rhythmic approach in a conversation in Paris: 'What Parker and Gillespie did harmonically and melodically, is already there in Bach and Beethoven. What really was new was the rhythm. Because I relaxed the hardness of the swing rhythm and liberated the beat, their ideas could first be realized.' In this connection one must not forget that this rhythmic scheme was foreshadowed in Kansas

Monk with Dizzy Gillespie

City swing, which Clarke and Monk had both experienced at first hand.

The beat was not only liberated at the drum set, the piano also helped free it from the fetters of a regular, measure-by-measure conformity. The bass, with its now audible, supple tone, became the new 'slave to the rhythm', but could even consider this role empowering, since it now set the pace for the rhythmic and harmonic progressions.

As regards piano accompaniment, an essential consideration was that it was spare, that it often sat out whole measures, the better to contribute contrasting accents keyed to the harmonic changes. Dizzy Gillespie, with an inventor's pride, claims to have introduced all pianists to this style of accompaniment. We should note, however, that in essence it is analogous to Clarke's style of drumming, and so can be considered instead another product of Minton's rhythm team. After all, Dizzy Gillespie wrote on the photo of himself that he dedicated to Monk, and which decorated Monk's piano from the late forties on: 'To Thelonious Monk. My first inspiration. Stay with it. Your boy, Dizzy Gillespie.'

Thelonious Monk conceived of accompaniment not only as a process of contributing harmonic highlights, but also as an opportunity to shape the underlying form. In bebop it is customary to treat the theme as merely harmonic scaffolding. The theme is heard in full before and after the parade of solos, while the soloists themselves often pay it scant attention. Not so with Thelonious Monk. Not only do the basic motifs of the theme appear in his solos, but he also avails himself explicitly of the thematic material in his accompaniment. Thus the whole number is of a thematic piece.

In stark contrast, it is true, stands a method of accompaniment that reduces the spareness of bebop accompaniment to virtual non-accompaniment. Monk increasingly cultivated this for whole choruses, with the simple explanation that a piano-less rhythm section produced a whole new world of sound especially in the horns, a world he particularly liked.

In his solos performed in a combo setting, Thelonious traveled a path few other pianists have taken. The new support of the bass and drums did not encourage him to assign the harmonic signposts to the left hand, while reserving the melody to the right—a technique his protégé Bud Powell was to develop into a style all his own. With Monk the newly empowered rhythm section led to a still more concentrated economy of expression, and to the indiscriminate use of the right and left hand. Again, we have to reckon with the influence of Kansas City, and Count Basie in particular. In Monk's case, sounds are distributed between either hand, which sometimes operate independently, sometimes in coordination to produce block chords dominated by the ninth interval. In the bass, the ninths are sometimes shortened to seconds. To be sure, the two-handed style is sometimes suspended altogether, not, however, in favor of hornlike melodic lines, but in order to startle the listener with one-handed, minimal motifs that are starkly and percussively juxtaposed against the rhythmic flow.

When people say that few pianists followed Monk's example, that should not be taken to mean that Monk's influence as a pianist was negligible. It is true that many musicians and jazz critics pay unreserved tribute to Monk the composer, while claiming that his pianistic influence was slight. But there are pianists who contest this evaluation. The pianist Mal Waldron, who along with Herbie Nichols, Randy Weston, Cecil Taylor, and Richard Muhal Abrams—to name only the most prominent musicians—made pilgrimages to Minton's after the war, was emphatic when I questioned him on the subject: 'All the younger musicians loved him. He was not popular with the older musicians. The younger musicians felt that he was into something that was different. If people liked his compositions they liked his playing. His playing was accepted. It was very strange sounding, very different sounding. Everybody was into being different at that time. And we looked up to Monk, because he was more different than anybody else. And that was the keynote to jazz: to be different, to have your own personality.'

Cecil Taylor confirms the influence that Monk exercised upon him: 'It was also the realization of some things that I learned from Monk–that is, the placement of the chords in relation to the bass and drums, especially the bass, the steady element. Monk plays very subtly, more subtly than the eighth-note playing of the boogie-woogie pianists and some of the younger players. As a result, he can jar you emotionally. A horn player playing with Monk must think faster, must think instantly, and Monk does not overblow. That was something I was working on around that time.'

'Bags' Groove'

THE 'BAGS' GROOVE' – 'THE MAN I LOVE' RECORDINGS MADE ON Christmas Eve, 1954 document Monk's qualities as an ensemble pianist in exemplary fashion. Among Miles Davis' works these recordings are also often hailed as high points of improvisatory art. One illustrious critic of Monk, André Hodeir, sees in his solo on 'Bags' Groove' 'a moment of purest beauty in the history of jazz.' For me, also, 'Bags' Groove' represents one of the most perfect performances of ensemble jazz.

The personnel itself was a stroke of especially good luck for Monk, even if the recordings bear the unmistakable stamp of the leader, Miles Davis. The trumpeter in his early years belonged to the regular patrons at Monk's 'house seminars.' After the recording sessions, he would also spend the rest of the day in Monk's home. The same goes for the vibraphonist Milt Jackson, whose wealth of melodic, blues-inflected ideas Monk had increasingly relied on as a foil to his own odd, abrupt, subtly modulated phrases. In the rhythm section sat Kenny Clarke, the man who, in close collaboration with Monk, was responsible for the rhythmic concept of modern jazz. Finally, in Percy Heath you had a bassist who not only honored the new rhythmic responsibilities of the bass, but who also had absorbed the harmonic and melodic innovations of Oscar Pettiford and Ray Brown. With natural assurance and great sympathetic powers he was able to exploit the opportunity to create patterns of contrapuntal bass lines. Seldom does one have the chance later to hear Monk play with so creative a bassist.

Obviously, The 'Jazz Giants' who were united for this recording session were deeply marked by Monk's musical ideas, so that, for the time being at least, they formed a more musically coherent ensemble than many playing at the time. The tensions in the studio are in that regard no contradiction, and at bottom of no importance. It has been reported that Miles Davis compelled Monk to sit out the sessions after 'The Man I Love' and 'Bemsha Swing.' Others believe that Monk resorted to his often attested practice of deliberate non-accompaniment. Kenny Clarke, in reviewing the whole controversy, will only say by way of personal reminiscence that Monk, during Davis' solos, actually had to excuse himself to go to the bathroom, and that he was notorious for getting his way.

But what makes the first take of 'Bags' Groove' so special? The theme by Milt 'Bags' Jackson, essentially a simple, repeated, four-bar blues riff, is already part of the answer. It sounds earthy, bluesy, and yet entirely modern and open. It is this 'open' quality that Miles Davis brings out in a solo of abstract, ground-breaking logic. After Miles' solo, Milt Jackson, with vibrant imagination, highlights the earthy, bluesy element, which, thanks in part to the sound of his instrument, does not clash with the coolness of Davis. Monk at the piano elaborates on Jackson's ideas with blues chords that sound, with their tendency toward atonality, as if they were hardening into abstraction.

In his solo Monk first devises in a tight, swinging rhythm a two-note motif against the breathing beat of bass and drums, then develops it over the course of two choruses. In the third chorus this development undergoes a tonal and rhythmic expansion that excites tense expectation. In the fourth chorus this tension is relieved with a series of rhythmically capricious chord clusters of a deeply probing character that test the limits of tonality. The piano hints at an underlying 'three against four' movement. The contrapuntally operating walking bass, anchored steadfastly four-to-the-bar, answers at the end of the chorus with a three against four phrase. Thus it functions as more than a ground foil, it heightens the rhythmic tension in a new way.

Again, Kenny Clarke, who unlike the otherwise so competent Art Blakey, never yielded to the temptation to comment on the surface structure of Monk's rhythmic patterns, punctuates with spare accents the deep structure of the overall rhythm. He highlights the moments when the phrasing of the piano intersects with the counterpoint of the bass. With good reason Max Roach once called Kenny Clarke 'the Thelonious Monk of drummers.'

After this tension-laden *tour de force* Monk, in an abrupt departure, switches to the use of the right hand that avails itself only sporadically of support from the left. He returns, with rhythmic variations, to elements found in his playing of the second chorus. Pauses function as dramatic elements; triplet phrases are heard by implication without actually being voiced. Ever more bizarre downward leaps heighten the sense of tension, which is also enhanced by percussive, note-bending effects. Miles Davis' three choruses before the reprise—again accompanied only by bass and percussion—strive in their entirety for a classical balance of strictly horizontal logic, simmering blues vitality, and vertical, harshly percussive blues motifs. It is fortunate that, by the end of 1954, recording techniques had advanced to the point where a track was produced satisfying even for listeners on today's sophisticated stereo equipment.

Both takes of 'The Man I Love' illustrate in an extreme form Monk's technique of playing the theme melody, with daring variations of its note values, as a solo. Milt Jackson doubles the tempo after the trumpet solo. The rhythm section maintains double time through Monk's solo. In the A-section he plays the substance of the theme as displaced elements in the original slow tempo, thus creating an effect of augmentation. With the rhythmic and har-

monic tensions his specific treatment of the theme melody becomes at once the creator and accompanist of a silently played
solo of implications, that are only made explicit by the piano in
the B-section. In the bass, too, rhythmic tension is created through
counterpoint. Kenny Clarke proves once again that he was the
ideal percussionist for Monk, with the way he grasps the underlying rhythmic structure. It is unfortunate that, before he moved to
Paris in 1956, he only appeared in the studio with Monk on one
other occasion.

Monk with Kenny Dorham in the early fifties

The Composer

'THELONIOUS MONK IS AN EXTRAORDINARY EXAMPLE OF A CREATIVE talent who is corrupted by nothing. He has accepted all the challenges that one must accept if one wants to create music in the jazz idiom. Because he was, perhaps fortunately, not exposed to the tradition of classical western music, or for that matter to anything but jazz and American popular music, he created a unique and astoundingly pure music by utilizing their external forms, supporting them with deeper structures.' No less a figure than the pianist Bill Evans (who some may regard as the antithesis of Thelonious Monk) has expressed his admiration for the creations of his colleague in these words.

The general recognition of Thelonious Monk as composer preceded by over fifteen years his recognition as a pianist. His composition "Round Midnight' was played by the trumpeter Cootie Williams' big band, even before the Minton days. To be sure, Williams used his own B-section in order to collect royalties. But for the beboppers, too, Monk's compositions soon attained the status of standards. They played 'Fifty-Second Street Theme', and in general took great interest in what he wrote. Gil Fuller, arranger for Dizzy Gillespie's big band, reports how eager he and Dizzy were to keep him in the band for the sake of his compositions–and this despite Monk's rather broadly conceived idea of start-up times, and his general unreliability. (In fact, these factors were to finally outweigh their eagerness to retain him.)

Up until October 1952, Monk's repertoire consisted of twenty-three of his own titles, of which 'Epistrophy', 'Straight, No Chaser', and 'Well, You Needn't' in particular attained the status of standards. In his following three years with the Prestige label he added sixteen more originals; of these 'Bemsha Swing' and 'Blue Monk' became standards. In the subsequent seven years with Riverside the number of originals decreased to thirteen, among them the classics 'Brilliant Corners' and 'Crepuscule with Nellie.' But these are so stamped with Monk's musical personality that in his lifetime few others ventured to play them. Increasingly, Monk revived and played old compositions, and the number of originals produced in his CBS years, from 1962 to 1967, shrank to ten.

Bill Evans' remarks apply to Monk's themes in the sense that, almost without exception, all are either in the twelve-bar blues form, or in the traditional thirty-two bar song form. What makes these simply some of the best known themes in jazz, is that Monk was able, working within these parameters, to achieve thoroughly unique and masterful results. When you first hear a Monk composition in AABA form, it is immediately clear that the B-section is a dominant element in the whole theme. Monk's choice of language is revealing here: while the B-section is often called the 'bridge', and in fact often serves only as a device to get back to the A-section, for Monk it represents what he called 'the *inside* of the composition.'

His blues numbers are also more than the usual four-bar riffs. Even when they are constructed that simply, the rhythmic displacements always ensure that an over-arching thematic structure results. Günter Buhles has shown in the case of 'Straight, No Chaser' how Monk plays with the possibilities for structural recombination inherent in the form. The theme can be analyzed as either a generic twelve-bar asymmetric blues theme in the bop tradition, or as two symmetrical, six-bar motifs, linked in AB form.

What is special about all Monk's tunes, and what is so fascinatingly elusive and entrancing about them, is their peculiar sense of rhythm. The key lies in what Monk said in his blindfold test about 'Rhythm-a-ning': 'The piece swings by itself. To keep with the song, you have to swing.'

On 'Criss Cross'—for many Monk fans his most perfect piece—this innate swing is shown to best effect. The whole tune basically consists of two motifs, each having the character of a kind of melodic shorthand. The first is an embellished descending flatted fifth taking up the time of one beat, but because of the embellishment actually occurring off the beat. In the four-bar piano introduction of the Blue Note recording, there is no accent note to relieve the tension created by the interval of the flatted fifth. In the second bar we do have a release note, in the form of a pure ascending fifth on the offbeat of two. Consequently, the thematic shorthand motif now appears on the four, pushing the accented note of the following bar on the 'square' downbeat, but now as a weird—or better say 'hip'—raised fifth.

Now the shorthand motif is on the relatively strong third beat, and on the weak fourth beat there is a real release with an accent in the form of a sixth. In the fourth measure, finally, the motif is on the second beat, and its accent comes on the third beat as a minor seventh—in jazz a neutral interval suggestive of harmonic openness. It correlates with the rhythmically neutral third beat, which is not really weak, but not the downbeat either. The cycle of shifting accents with its correlated intervals and their tonal tensions comes full circle on the downbeat at the beginning of the A-section.

This description may be enough to show how brilliantly tonal tension and rhythmic displacement are interwoven, creating symmetry by cyclical rhythmic progression. The accented note occurs on each of the four beats in chromatic progression, its tonal value being in constant opposition to the rhythmic value or strength of the beat in question. Here it is time to stop and con-

sider that the phenomenon of swing has been described as a result of 'the conflict between a fixed pulse and the wide variety of
actual durations and accents that a jazz performer plays against
that pulse.' This is the more effective in 'Criss Cross' because the
quaver-rest in the first bar (the 'zero accent', to give it a name)
stretches the time, and by the same token is responsible for a
cyclic rhythmic super-imposition of three against four. And with
the cycle coming to completion after the first four bars, the whole
intro acquires the coherence of a miniature overture. (The fact
that Monk in his later recordings resorted to different introduc-
tions will be discussed after a look at the theme itself.)

By analogy with what was said about the intro, the first four
bars of the A-section can be seen as a prelude to what is, in effect,
the main motif of the whole piece: the reiterated diminishing jumps
downward to the first step (if the piece is interpreted as in G minor, but with typical Monk ambivalence it can also be interpreted
as being in B minor, in which case G becomes the sixth step),
resulting from the chromatic progression of the top notes in the
jumping string of eighth notes starting with F″. The chromaticism
of the accent notes of the introduction already revolved around
this first (sixth) step. It is true that this chromaticism is dropped in
the actual A-section, thus suggesting a certain release. Yet the chromaticism of the intro continues to be felt, and now its implied
expectations are fulfilled in the leaping intervals of bars five and
following, making these intervals the main thematic material of
the tune, all the more since they, too, in analogy with the intro,
undergo the same rhythmic and tonal progression.

Three against four was a key term. In the B-section we have a
different grouping in three. The main motif, derived from the
main thematic material of bar five of the A-section, extends over
three bars, and this group of three is repeated once. The first interval of this main thematic material, however, is modulated to a
sixth, and the movement of the motif steers toward a halt on the

fifth step. This fifth step naturally demands repetition of the whole three-bar-grouping, and the demand is met, as we saw. Yet the equally classical song form requires two more bars. Monk comes up with a crazy but ingenious solution: a tonality-blurring run downwards to the flatted sixth, creating a false relation, after which the return to the A-section brings a welcome release. In later recordings Monk dropped these two bars. This yields a more coherent tune, underlying the importance Monk attached to a song's B-section. On the CBS *Criss Cross* record Monk abridges the intro to two bars, and his Black Lion recording has bars five and following of the A-section as an intro. Both procedures highlight in their way the importance of the 'inside of the composition.'

We saw how Monk uses the traditional song form, one of the 'external forms' Bill Evans spoke of, as a vehicle for his 'deeper structures', yielding 'a unique and astoundingly pure music.' One of his compositional methods has aptly been called 'montage technique' by the musicologist Peter Niklas Wilson. A minimum of two motifs assembled in at least two patterns creates a maximum of effect. The other essential aspects of 'Monkishness' identified by Wilson are also evident in the classic 'Criss Cross': the reduction of musical 'space', the renunciation of obvious virtuosity, and—as attention to the bass notes of the left hand will show, when compared with the implications of the chord symbols—'harmonic thinning.'

That 'harmonic thinning', combined with Monk's typically angular piano sound, is the reason why even his most emotional ballads never sound overly sentimental, let alone saccharine—at least in his own renditions. The jazz critic Whitney Balliet had something else to add: 'His improvisations were molten compositions, and his compositions were frozen Monk improvisations.' Either way, both are the result of a peculiarly pianistic approach to music. Monk's compositions are primarily works for piano, for Monk's piano to be precise; and it is interesting that he never recorded the blowing line themes that he wrote at the beginning of his career (e.g. 'Fifty-Second Street Theme'), or did not record them after his Blue Note years (e.g. 'Humph').

This particular character of Monk's compositions explains why not very many musicians venture to play them, even today. The most notable exception is the soprano saxophonist Steve Lacy. For years Lacy concentrated on Monk material, and he is among the very few who have managed to interpret his tunes in both a personal and a Monkish way—without in the least producing what might be called a pastiche.

PART 3

MONK'S CATALOG

Music on Disc

ONLY A FEW YEARS AGO, it was relatively difficult to obtain certain recordings by Thelonious Monk. Today, in the wake of the much-publicized jazz revival, it is possible to get all Monk's Blue Note, Riverside, CBS, Black Lion, and Vogue recordings, in outstandingly remastered CD versions, often at a discount. The complete Blue Note recordings, originally available only from Mosaic, are now put out by Blue Note itself in a four-CD package. The complete London material of Black Lion and Vogue, also published by Mosaic, is now available from The Jazz Store (see Filmography) in a new edition by Black Lion. Riverside, too, has finally brought out a complete edition of their Monk recordings on fifteen CDs.

The classic albums with their original covers, now in CD form, continue to define Monk's work. This is the form in which his work will be discussed in this section. They will be listed with their original LP numbers, followed by the CD numbers. Where the CDs contain a bonus track, this will be noted. Where the discographic data is in doubt we rely on Michael Cuscuna (Mosaic Blue Note booklet) or Leon Bijl/Fred Canté. This survey is intended primarily to explore the musical and biographical aspects of Monk's recordings. The reader may refer to discographies listed in the bibliography for further information.

In what follows, only authorized recordings, with a few exceptions, are discussed. There exists a number of unauthorized broadcast recordings of the Monk quartet on tour, owing to the fact that most concerts were produced in cooperation with radio stations. These recordings are often of poor technical quality and are easy to recognize because they list only the year of recording by way of a date. The Affinity recordings from 1966 are in this category, and are included here only with the greatest reservation. *Thelonious Monk 1963 in Japan* also falls into this category.

The live recordings from Minton's are a more complex case. They do not meet the definition of 'authorized recordings', and we can confine ourselves to recommending the following two collections to anyone with an interest in early Monk: Don Byas' *Midnight At Minton's* from 1941 (Onyx ORI-208; Musidisc/Jazz Anthology 5121), and a Xanadu recording, also from 1941, *Harlem Odyssey* (Xanadu 112). It is certain that Monk plays on both throughout. His playing is interesting in that, for all its conventional fluency, it is still unmistakably his. Joe Guy and Kenny Clarke also appear on both recordings.

The reviews of the Monk quartet recordings are deliberately kept short because these performances are often quite similar to one another, both in repertoire and in formal execution.

A list of the individual selections follows the name of the record and its catalog number. The selections are listed in the order in which they were originally recorded. Their description, however, follows the sequence on the original LP. The personnel, along with the recording date, are listed before the different selections.

Since the first edition of this book, several authorized, previously unreleased Monk recordings have appeared. Most are live recordings of the quartet on tour. They are mentioned here in the appropriate places with selections, personnel and recording dates. But we only go into the music when it departs significantly from Monk's usual concert repertoire.

Where a recording date is given that differs from the one on the album or CD jacket, the date given here is one that research has found to be correct. So far as possible, references to the CD versions (inclusive of bonus tracks) have been added. All the original Columbia/CBS records have appeared on CD with their original covers, and, in a few cases, with additional selections.

Coleman Hawkins Quartet
Bean and the Boys
Prestige PR 7824; CD 24124-2

Coleman Hawkins (ts), Monk (p), Edward 'Bass' Robinson (b), Denzil Best (d); October 19, 1944:
FLYING HAWK / DRIFTIN' ON A REED / ON THE BEAN / RECOLLECTIONS

These are the first official recordings of Thelonious Monk, and he makes an outstanding first impression. He was later the terror of many hornplayers, but here he supports his leader in a co-operative spirit. He plays the chord changes clearly, reminding one of Dodo Marmarosa of the Charlie Parker Quintet. Also reminiscent of Marmarosa are the brief intros that Monk plays on every piece.

In 'On the Bean' he has a sixteen-bar solo. His right hand plays blowing lines to a conventional bop accompaniment in the left; only Monk's preferred intervals are distinctive. 'Recollections' and 'Driftin' On a Reed' are ballads and, as such, pure Hawkins features. One thing to note is that on 'Driftin'' Monk plays the beginning of 'I'm Getting Sentimental Over You', another ballad that he would later record repeatedly. On 'Flying Hawk' he ventures on a whole chorus. Here again he surprises us with his fast blowing lines, but the sound is unmistakably Monk, not least because in the bridge and the ensuing A-section he quotes 'Well, You Needn't' at length. Coleman Hawkins bursts with ideas on all the numbers. His phrasing, however, remains true to his style. Bass and drums play light and open, 'four-to-the-bar.'

These four numbers were originally issued on two 78 RPM shellacks with the Joe Davis label. Both LP and CD editions of this recording include other tracks on which Monk does not appear, all by Coleman Hawkins octets.

The Blue Note Years

The advent of CD versions has created some confusion about Monk's first releases with Blue Note. On the two original *Genius of Modern Music* LPs the distribution of selections is different than on the corresponding CDs. The CDs are arranged chronologically, and include two selections that were left off the originals.

The discussion below is based on the arrangement of the original LP releases. A description of the CD reissues follows, with notes on the additional selections.

Genius of Modern Music: Volume 1
Blue Note BLP 1510

Idrees Sulieman (tp), Danny Quebec West (as), Billy Smith (ts), Monk (p), Gene Ramey (b), Art Blakey (d); October 15, 1947:
HUMPH / THELONIOUS
Without Sulieman, West, or Smith; October 24, 1947:
OFF MINOR / RUBY, MY DEAR / WELL, YOU NEEDN'T / APRIL IN PARIS / INTROSPECTION
George Taitt (tp), Sahib Shihab (as), Monk (p), Bob Paige (b), Art Blakey (d); November 21, 1947:
IN WALKED BUD / 'ROUND MIDNIGHT
Milt Jackson (vib), Monk (p), John Simmons (b), Shadow Wilson (d); July 2, 1948:
MYSTERIOSO / EPISTROPHY / I MEAN YOU

The owners of Blue Note embarked on the production of their 'discovery', Thelonious Monk, with great enthusiasm. They recorded him in October and November of 1947, and again in July 1948, more copiously than could be accommodated on their 78 RPM disks. With this overabundance of material, and in view of the poor sales of Monk's records, Blue Note subsequently put on the brakes. They did not return Monk to the studio until July of 1951 and May 1952.

The series 'Genius of Modern Music' does not adhere to the original chronology; the two albums present a selection from the entire output of this earlier period. Again, the pieces are listed in the chronological order in which they were recorded; the discussions conform to the sequence of titles on the records.

The 78 RPM format of the original Blue Note releases imposed an arbitrary limit on the length of the numbers. One consequence is that on pieces in AABA song form the soloists often share in a chorus, or the reprise of the theme begins immediately after a partial chorus. Many numbers have a compelling terseness as a result. *Genius of Modern Music* begins with the best known of all his compositions, ''Round Midnight', which has become the anthem of classic modern jazz. The quintet plays a subtle variation on the introduction that Dizzy Gillespie prefixed to his performance of this ballad in 1946, and which became a standard feature of the composition ever after. Monk states the theme of the A-section, accompanied by the horns. His voice moves upward in brief, contrasting phases. The B-section is improvised by Monk while the horns play behind him. Twice he throws in his brilliant whole tone runs. In the third A-section Monk is free to do what he wants at the piano; he appends eight measures of an harmonically adventuresome solo. The drums lend extra excitement to the unusually fast ballad tempo by hinting at double time. In the second A-section of the piano chorus, the horns again come in with their parallel lines, and there is no reprise of the theme. By way of a coda Monk plays a descending arpeggio extending over several octaves; this was retained in all Monk's subsequent performances of the piece. Precisely because the well known theme is not played in its regular form, but merely serves as a foil for the succession of

Monk's forceful, condensed phrases, this is one of the most beautiful performances of the number recorded.

'Off Minor', a piece in medium tempo, is a beautiful example of Monk's unique and masterly way with song form. A four-bar descending motif undergoes a subtle variation in the second half, leading naturally to a repetition of the A-section. The B-section parallels in one single melodic movement the direction of the A-section motif, that with the reprise emphasizes the coherence of the whole piece. Monk's solo ingeniously fragments the rhythm, harmony, and melody of the tune. It leads forcefully to the reprise, which this time dispenses with the B-section.

Monk's ballad 'Ruby, My Dear' is also in song form. It has a more idiosyncratic charm than "Round Midnight.' In his solo Monk elaborates on the A-section with unusual intervals; the reprise is also limited to the A-section. Virtuosic pianistic effects, including a descending whole tone run followed by an ascending arpeggio accompanied by dense chord clusters in the left hand, bring the piece to a close. Here, as in all the pieces described thus far, the rhythm section lends supple support, and Art Blakey is especially clever and congenial.

On 'I Mean You', played in a faster bounce tempo, we hear Monk in an entirely different setting. Monk's friend and Count Basie drummer Shadow Wilson contributes a more evenly swinging, but no less interesting accompaniment. And in Milt Jackson Monk had a lively, horizontally-oriented foil. Despite its song form, this Monk composition has a funky, bluesy character. This may explain why Gerry Mulligan would later not only perform the piece, but pass it off as his own under the title 'Motel.' In the B-section Jackson and Monk play off one another in a stimulating exchange. Jackson and Monk share a solo chorus, and it is interesting how Monk's angular and not very supportive accompaniment does not put Jackson off from his almost swing-style solo.

Monk's own solo plays with ideas in quasi-arpeggio form. 'April in Paris', again with the same rhythm section as on the first number, is conventional by Monk's standards. Despite his characteristic piano style, the somewhat commonplace harmonies of the basic theme remain predominant.

'In Walked Bud', on the other hand, captures Monk at his most distinctive. With a descending whole tone run performed *con brio* he dramatizes his friend Powell 'walking in.' Then the ensemble joins in with the fanfare-like theme in song form, which contrasts with the B-section, though it too has a fanfare-like flavor. Monk's rhythmically and harmonically unsettling piano accents became a standard element of this classic Monk composition. In his solo he plays a kind of ping-pong with Art Blakey, in which rhythmic and melodic shreds of the theme serve as the bouncing ball. George Taitt plays a half-chorus on the trumpet, which in tone and phrasing harks back to the swing era. Sahib Shihab's alto saxophone, next, is pure bebop, but in a style independent of Charlie Parker.

'Thelonious' is Monk's famous 'monotone theme' in medium-fast tempo. The theme's single note is sufficient to create music, because of the way harmony and rhythm are juxtaposed to the ever-shifting accents of this note, as the piano in the A-section hammers it out in Morse code fashion. The harmonic contrasts provided by the horns are particularly striking here. In the expanded B-section, the piano plays around this tone, then demonstrates again in the A-section that it has it firmly in its grasp. Monk is the only soloist. His solo begins with a spare structure similar to that of the theme itself. In the second chorus Monk's left hand suddenly begins to comp in stride style, while the right continues its explorations up and down the keyboard. There is a rhythmically brilliant passing reference to the theme of 'Salt Peanuts.' The reprise is again composed of the A-section.

The quartet with Milt Jackson reappears on 'Epistrophy', the melody that Monk had developed from a motif by Kenny Clarke. (Later it would become the quartet's theme music.) The basic motif sounds like a drum theme proceeding upward from the bass drum over the tom-toms, and then, nudged by the bass drum, moving downward again over the tom-toms. Against this figure Monk juxtaposes bursts of ascending triplets in the bass. Shadow Wilson holds the contrary movements together with his work on the hi-hat, which reminds one of Jo Jones. In the B-section the vibraphone swings straightforwardly, but the bass in the piano does not cease its dark menacing, and so Jackson is more reserved in the second A-section. During his logical solo the piano again picks out contrasts. After sixteen measures it goes its sullen way for the rest of the chorus. The hi-hat continues to hold tight to the rhythmic reins.

'Mysterioso' is yet another Monk classic. Intervals of a sixth, in eighth notes, are picked out step-wise upwards and downwards through the blues scale. The bass half of the piano increasingly contrasts with the vibraphone descant. In its solo the vibraphone swings softly, while the piano lays down widely spaced chords darkened by dissonance. It is along the lines established by these probing chords that the piano in its first chorus seeks out new material. The second chorus follows the rhythmic pattern of the theme, to become less mysterious, even cheerful, finally ending in a rapid arpeggio. The theme, reprised on the vibraphone, is also bright in mood. Only at the very end does it become complicated again by bass notes from the piano.

'Well, You Needn't' is performed in a trio setting. It is among the few melodies by Monk that other musicians have played with any frequency. It is a masterful example of how Monk constructed coherent up-tempo themes in AABA form from shorthand motifs and a compelling B-section. In the middle of Monk's solo there is an interesting passage of chord clusters. 'Well, You Needn't' is one of the Monk themes that, in his own words, 'swings by itself.'

The debut performances on Blue Note of the compositions he had written to this date are generally among his best. But there are certainly later versions of 'Well, You Needn't' that are better than this one.

'Introspection' in medium-fast tempo, is a Monk composition in expanded song-form. The melody, too, sounds songful and rather melancholy. But if you try to hum it you soon discover how unconventional it is. In his solo Monk hews closely to the melody and illuminates it with various sound-colors. He does not, however, fragment it or subject it to his typically trenchant analysis.

With 'Humph' at the end we have a Monk piece that in tempo and blowing-line structure is clearly in the bebop tradition. It is probably no coincidence that it was the first side Monk ever recorded for Blue Note. Danny Quebec West had thoroughly studied his Parker, and Idrees Sulieman his Dizzy Gillespie. Billy Smith, for his part, sounds like Dexter Gordon. In his solo Monk takes the theme apart in uncharacteristically fluent, legato figures that nevertheless bear his unmistakable signature.

Genius of Modern Music: Volume 2
Blue Note BLP 1511

Idrees Sulieman (tp), Danny Quebec West (as), Billy Smith (ts), Monk (p), Gene Ramey (b), Art Blakey (d); October 15, 1947:
EVONCE / SUBURBAN EYES
Without Sulieman, West, or Smith; October 21, 1947:
NICE WORK IF YOU CAN GET IT
George Taitt (tp), Sahib Shihab (as), Monk (p), Bob Paige (b), Art Blakey (d); November 21, 1947:
MONK'S MOOD / WHO KNOWS?
Sahib Shihab (as), Milt Jackson (vib), Monk (p), Al McKibbon (b), Art Blakey (d); July 23, 1951:
FOUR IN ONE / STRAIGHT, NO CHASER / ASK ME NOW
Kenny Dorham (tp), Lou Donaldson (as), Lucky Thompson (ts), Monk

(p), Nelson Boyd (b), Max Roach (d); May 30, 1952:
SKIPPY / LET'S COOL ONE / CAROLINA MOON /
HORNIN' IN

This record makes a somewhat equivocal impression, at least on me. The first three pieces represent the last recordings that Monk made for Blue Note as a bandleader. The context is that of a sextet, whose possibilities Monk sought to exploit with thoroughly planned head arrangements. There are statements by him at the time to the effect that the sextet was his favorite setting. And yet the performances only intermittently attain to the definitive quality that distinguishes those on *Vol. 1* and always makes them sound so fresh. That goes especially for 'Carolina Moon.' After the brief but promising piano intro, the Tin Pan Alley style pop song is subjected to an arrangement unique for the time: it is presented in 6/4 tempo with headlong eighth notes. The horns improvise briefly over this rhythm. Monk's accompaniment is rather conventional, and his eight-bar solo is none too exciting either. With the reprise of the A-section the piece comes to an abrupt end. The rhythmic daring of this piece seems rather tame today, when experiments with unconventional time signatures are common.

The leader's 'Hornin' In' is a grooving, mid-tempo number in AABA form. It has Monk's distinctive harmonies, but does not venture much beyond the conventions of bebop. Kenny Dorham plays a relaxed solo, whose tone, which owes more to early Miles Davis than to Gillespie, is heard to good advantage. Lucky Thompson contributes a robust yet fluent tenor solo. The brief contribution of Lou Donaldson is very simply conceived. Again, Monk's accompaniment is surprisingly smooth and self-effacing. His solo, in turn, is uncharacteristically horn-like. The reprise, again, consists of the A-section only.

'Skippy' starts with the piano soloing over the first twenty-four bars of the 32-bar ABA'C structure. The close-knit interplay between Monk and Max Roach, executed in a fast jump tempo, is highly sophisticated, and prepares for the C-section with its downward and then upward movement, eventually culminating in a strident signal motif. Lucky Thompson plays an earthy solo reminiscent of Coleman Hawkins. Kenny Dorham skillfully picks up some of Thompson's ideas, which in turn are developed and judiciously distorted by Monk in his chorus. The bass voice of the piano, which has repeatedly harked back to the rhythmic structure of the opening chorus, now assumes a life of its own in contrast to the fraying lines of the upper register. A distinct chord progression leads to the full statement of the theme by the horns: a string of boppish motifs that abruptly yields to the C-section already known. The whole take is a masterpiece of Monkiana.

'Let's Cool One' is performed in a moderate bounce tempo. The readily hummable tune is simply construed by Monk, leaving room at the breaks for drum solos. The trumpet plays a subdued chorus in a singing tone. Lou Donaldson plays a similarly conservative half chorus, which Lucky Thompson completes with masterful ease. Monk contributes a beautiful example of his playing with fragmented motifs. The bass walks his solo over the B-section, before everybody comes in on the last A-section of the chorus for the reprise. The piece breaks off with a short drum coda, the same drum fill, in fact, that has already completed bars seven and eight of the initial A-sections.

'Suburban Eyes' by Ike Quebec, with its unison horn lines, is classic uptempo bebop. Danny Quebec West plays a superb alto solo. Idrees Sulieman's solo is fluent enough, but he gets somewhat entangled in the middle. Monk's solo foreshadows the peculiar shorthand style of his, which, with its harmonic and rhythmic intricacies, was later to become one of his trademarks. It is this shorthand style that throws new light on the theme, adding a Monkish tinge when it is restated.

The bebop theme 'Evonce' by Ike Quebec and Idrees Sulieman receives similar treatment. Sulieman is confident playing over his own theme. Smith and Monk confine themselves to brief, straightforward solos. 'Straight, No Chaser' is famous from many jam sessions, where it serves well as a blues blowing vehicle. Its composer takes it at medium tempo. In essence it consists of a simple, subtly modulated motif. Its subtlety can be better appreciated at this moderate speed. Art Blakey's drum introduction sets the pace. The piano presents the theme in an introductory chorus, before it is taken up by the ensemble. Monk's piano solo highlights the latent refinement of the theme. He hands it off to the alto sax with a quotation from 'Mysterioso.' Again one has cause to regret that Shihab later abandoned the alto for the baritone saxophone. Next, Milt Jackson plays with his usual, lively blues feeling, and is accompanied by Monk with spare contrasts. Al McKibbon's bass sounds livelier than that of his colleagues on this disk. The same personnel plays Monk's shimmering 'Four In One' in a similar tempo. Monk's solo plays with the outlines of the melody. It creates a tranquil mood, which is taken up by Shihab, then maintained by Jackson in the course of a slowly developing vibe solo. In the reprise the melody seems less to shimmer than to darkly sparkle.

Gershwin's 'Nice Work' is performed in a trio setting, and subjected to the typical Monk process of recomposition. It is performed up-tempo, and enriched with various odd harmonic dissonances. A light stride touch allows it to swing as it should. 'Monk's Mood' is another one of those sweet-and-sour, melancholy Monk ballads in song form. The ensemble presents the theme. As if he wanted to highlight the sober, logical side of the piece, Monk begins his eight bar solo by quoting the B-section. Blakey hints at double time, and with a reprise of the A-section the piece concludes. 'Who Knows' again bops in quite traditional fashion—at least for a Monk tune. George Taitt in his solo shows some unsureness, which, however, is compensated for by Monk's fine solo. Blakey plays with a powerful drive. Shihab bops through the changes using shards of the melody, and Art Blakey permits himself a closing flourish on the drums after the reprise is through. Monk introduces 'Ask Me Now' with his beloved arpeggios. This is a typical Monk ballad in song form, presented here with only a very brief solo that works variations on the theme. It ends with a reprise of the A-section.

The arrangement of the *Genius Of Modern Music* CD reissues is as follows, including two additional selections: 'Sixteen' and 'I'll Follow You':

Genius of Modern Music: Volume 1
Blue Note 781510

HUMPH / EVONCE (2 takes) / SUBURBAN EYES (2 takes) / THELONIOUS / NICE WORK IF YOU CAN GET IT (2 takes) / RUBY, MY DEAR (2 takes) / WELL, YOU NEEDN'T (2 takes) / APRIL IN PARIS (2 takes) / OFF MINOR / INTROSPECTION / IN WALKED BUD / MONK'S MOOD / WHO KNOWS? (2 takes) / 'ROUND MIDNIGHT

Genius of Modern Music: Volume 2
Blue Note 781511

FOUR IN ONE (2 takes) / ERONEL / STRAIGHT, NO CHASER / ASK ME NOW (2 takes) / WILLOW WEEP FOR ME / SKIPPY (2 takes) / HORNIN' IN (2 takes) / SIXTEEN (2 takes) / CARO-LINA MOON / LET'S COOL ONE / I'LL FOLLOW YOU

'Sixteen' and 'I'll Follow You' both derive from the May 30, 1952 session. 'Sixteen' consists of dissonant, whirling, asymmetrical bebop motifs, above the harmonic structure of Sonny Rollins' 'Doxy.' The tempo, like that of its prototype, is a medium bounce. 'I'll Follow You' was a hit in 1932. Monk handles it in a trio setting. The way he plays with the theme and motifs anticipates his later wilder and more irreverent treatment of popular songs.

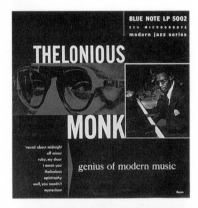

From top: Monk's first official recording, *Coleman Hawkins,*
Bean & the Boys; the original cover of *Genius of Modern Music;*
and the four CD set of Monk's complete Blue Note recordings.

Thelonious Monk / Milt Jackson
Blue Note 61012

*Kenny Pancho Hagood (voc), Milt Jackson (vib), Monk (p), John
Simmons (b), Shadow Wilson (d); July 2, 1948:*
ALL THE THINGS YOU ARE / I SHOULD CARE (2 takes)
*Sahib Shihab (as), Monk (p), Al McKibbon (b), Art Blakey (d); July
23 1951:*
CRISS CROSS (alternate take) / ASK ME NOW (alternate take)
*Milt Jackson (vib), Lou Donaldson (as), John Lewis (p), Percy Heath
(b), Kenny Clarke (d); April 7, 1952:*
WHAT'S NEW / DON'T GET AROUND MUCH ANYMORE (2
takes)

For a short time around 1985 these Blue Note discs, from Japan,
were available in Europe. In Japan there was a companion disc
available, Blue Note 61001, that contained further alternate takes
from the Blue Note sessions. Blue Note 61012 is included here to
represent the 'Monk with singer' genre, since the other disc that
documents Monk as accompanist to a vocalist, *Frankie Passions
with Thelonious Monk Quintet* (Washington 303/304), is very difficult to find.

The present reissue contains the recordings that the Monk/
Milt Jackson quartet made in order to back up vocalist Kenny
Pancho Hagood. In the studio the vocal tracks were laid down
first. The singer never really appealed to European audiences,
but in the United States black baritones who sang with an affected
bel canto vibrato had a long tradition. One thinks of Billy Eckstein,
or the singers whom Duke Ellington occasionally brought with
him to Europe. 'All the Things You Are' is interesting because of
the sarcastic remarks that Jackson and Monk can be heard making in the introduction, before the singer enters; and because of
Jackson's masterly solo, before the singer returns and the piece
reverts to its rather saccharine mood. Both versions of 'I Should
Care' proceed pretty much in this same manner. The second is

the weaker of the two. Monk alone solos, and is unusually timid. 'Ask Me Now' is an alternate take of the performance that can be heard on *Genius of Modern Jazz.* It was not released originally because Monk's solo goes on rather long, and overran the limits of the 78 RPM format. In plan and execution, this version otherwise differs little from the original. 'Criss Cross' is likewise an alternate take. The earlier take was the first to be published (see the description of the following disc). As so often, the soloists on the second take reflexively revert to the ideas that came spontaneously before. Consequently the solos here are less compelling, but still of a high order.

Milt Jackson
Blue Note BLP 1509

Milt Jackson (vib), Monk (p), John Simmons (b), Shadow Wilson (d); July 2, 1948:
EVIDENCE / MYSTERIOSO (alternate take)
Milt Jackson (vib), Sahib Shihab (as), Monk (p), Al McKibbon (b), Art Blakey (d); July 23, 1951:
FOUR IN ONE (alternate take) / CRISS CROSS / ERONEL / WILLOW WEEP FOR ME (*without Shihab*)
Milt Jackson (vib), Lou Donaldson (as), John Lewis (p), Percy Heath (b), Kenny Clarke (d); April 7, 1952:
LILLIE / TAHITI / WHAT'S NEW / BAGS' GROOVE / ON THE SCENE / LILLIE (alternate take)

After the Milt Jackson/Thelonious Monk quartet had discharged its obligation to the singer Kenny Hagood with wit and style, they turned to the making of the quartet performances that produced the Monk classics 'Mysterioso' (later spelled with an 'i') and 'Evidence'–performances justly hailed by the critics. BLP 1509 opens with recordings by the Milt Jackson group with John Lewis. These are followed by the fruits of the 1951 recording date with Monk. The standard 'Willow Weep for Me' is a Milt Jackson feature mi-

nus Monk solo. Monk's accompaniment is relatively conservative. Milt Jackson exploits the chance for relaxed playing in a
stepped-up ballad tempo. As on all his Blue Note performances
with Monk, his attack here is more aggressive than it was to be
with the Modern Jazz Quartet.

'Criss Cross' has already been analyzed in detail in the second section of the book. After the statement of the theme Milt
Jackson plays a very fluent solo. Sahib Shihab's contribution is
less boppish, and darkened in a rather Monkish way. The composer fragments the thematic material laconically, but quite ge-
nially, over the lively bounce rhythm. This leads logically to the
reprise. Monk's 'Eronel' is in AABA form. It is taken in an energetic but not a rushing tempo. After the piano introduction follows the unison presentation of the theme on vibes and alto sax.
Monk then plays an entire chorus resolutely limited to a paraphrase of the theme. Shihab and Jackson share a chorus in relaxed bop style before the reprise. 'Mysterioso' is an alternate
take. The performance is similar to the master (BLP 1510), but
minor additions and embellishments (Monk plays a second chorus on his solo) dilute the concentration that somehow elevates
the master to classic status.

'Four in One' is another alternate take. Again it conforms to
the pattern of the master (BLP 1511), but the soloists play more
fluently here, with greater fire and self-assurance. 'Evidence' at
the time of recording must have been just written. The theme, in
any case, appears only in Monk's introduction. This Monk composition would later become famous under the name 'Justice' as
the theme music of Art Blakey's Jazz Messengers. After the introduction comes Milt Jackson's straightforwardly swinging vibe solo.
Monk's solo is darkly searching and menacing. Then comes a
passage of interplay between Monk and Jackson, that for Monk's
part increasingly relies on thematic motifs. Shadow Wilson supports the whole thing with a Basie-style swing beat.

Bird & Diz

Clef MGC 512; CD: Verve 831 133-2 (bonus tracks, see below)

Charlie Parker (as), Hank Jones (p), Ray Brown (b), Buddy Rich (d);
March or April 1950:
STAR EYES / BLUES (FAST) / I'M IN THE MOOD FOR LOVE
Dizzy Gillespie (tp), Charlie Parker (as), Monk (p), Curly Russell (b),
Buddy Rich (d); June 6, 1950:
BLOOMIDO / AN OSCAR FOR TREADWELL / MOHAWK /
MY MELANCHOLY BABY / LEAP FROG

To questions about the one time he recorded with Charlie Parker
and Dizzy Gillespie, Monk regularly responded that 'it was just
another recording date.' In fact the numbers on which Monk plays
are rather disappointing from a Monk fan's perspective. In addition to the bebop standard 'My Melancholy Baby', the quintet
plays unison-line compositions by Parker typical of bebop. Monk
is only a sideman here, advertised for publicity purposes as 'the
mysterious high priest of bebop.' Buddy Rich was also brought
on board as a calculated attraction. Producer Norman Granz later
defended the choice of Rich, saying that it was Parker's idea. In
any event, the big band drum star with his swing approach adapts
poorly to the frantic bebop style, despite his display of virtuosity
in the breaks. The bassist with his supple 'walk' makes up for
some of the drummer's deficiencies. Parker, too, is in good form
and doesn't let any of these things distract him.

'Mohawk' is taken in bounce tempo. Monk's accompaniment
is idiosyncratic in his usual way. Gillespie's solo is enlivened by a
bit of by-play with the piano. The brief piano solo, consisting of a
blues chorus, represents Monk at his best. Then comes the bass
with its regulation chorus, and so ends the parade of soloists. On
'My Melancholy Baby' the piano plays a rather dry introduction,
in anticipation of Parker's usual flashy presentation of the subject.
Gillespie clowns a bit with the melody. In his solo, Monk again
fragments the material, and Parker picks up on the idea in his

periphrastic reprise. 'Leap Frog' is an up-tempo bebop 'jump' number. Parker and Gillespie deliver an eight-bar chase, which Rich is also drawn into, before the piece comes to a compelling close. On up-tempo numbers Rich had a better feel for the pulse of the music, and refrains from his usual break in the big band, star-drummer manner.

The later Verve edition of this LP (under the title *Historical Encounter*, Verve/Barclay 3606) and the CD edition, include alternate takes of 'An Oscar for Treadwell', 'Mohawk', and 'Leap Frog', and two takes of 'Relaxin' with Lee.'

All Monk's Blue Note recordings, with alternate and breakdown takes, are now available on:

The Complete Blue Note Recordings
Blue Note CDP 830363 (4 CDs)

The Prestige Years

Thelonious Monk Trio
Prestige LP 7027; CD: OJC 010

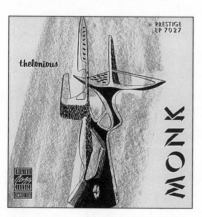

Monk (p), Gary Mapp (b), Art Blakey (d); October 15, 1952:
LITTLE ROOTIE TOOTIE / SWEET AND LOVELY / BYE-YA
/ MONK'S DREAM
Max Roach (d) replaces Art Blakey; December 18, 1952:
TRINKLE TINKLE/ THESE FOOLISH THINGS / BEMSHA
SWING / REFLECTIONS
Monk (p), Percy Heath (b), Art Blakey (d); September 22, 1954:
BLUE MONK
Monk (p)
JUST A GIGOLO

This disc collects the most important trio recordings that Monk
made for Prestige. It also documents Monk's debut with the label.
The first piece in the collection is Monk's celebrated blues 'Blue
Monk.' Like 'Straight, No Chaser', this piece, with its chromatic
movement, became a favorite of jam sessions. Monk himself takes
it in medium-fast tempo. The choruses are clearly structured and
defined. Blakey's accompaniment always illuminates Monk's soloing, which employs a wide range of devices, from single notes
in the right hand to two-handed clusters of block chords. Percy
Heath plays a spare, earthy solo, and Blakey follows with a contribution of disciplined energy, which leads naturally to the reprise (or was the reprise spliced on by the engineer?).

'Just a Gigolo' is a piano solo. Monk often performed this piece
alone. It is perhaps the most beautiful example of what has been
called his 'recomposition technique.' He plays with the thematic
motifs as with building blocks, and makes new connections between them with jump figures in the left hand. In the process he
devotes himself to the theme alone, accounting for the brevity of
his interpretation. On 'Blue Monk' and 'Just a Gigolo' Rudy Van
Gelder, the star among recording engineers, was at work, so the
sound quality is unsurpassed for its time.

'Bemsha Swing' sounds rather simple, but is characteristic
Monk with its 16-bar AABA structure and its deft references to
blues tonality and changes. It is powered by an Afro-Cuban per-

cussion figure. The poor engineering and out-of-tune piano of this studio date are regrettable. Monk performs his off-kilter interpretations in an especially declamatory manner, provoked by the disagreeable recording conditions. 'Reflections' is a beautiful medium-fast Monk song with typically shifting rhythmic and harmonic accents. Gary Mapp's bass playing beneath the leader's declamatory execution is solid, but falls short of the inventive elegance of Percy Heath, and Max Roach's snare figures are unfortunately hard to hear.

'Little Rootie Tootie' is dedicated to Monk's little son 'Toot.' Dad has paradoxically captured the rollicking spirit of his offspring by adhering to the strict structural limitations of the song form. After each four-bar phrase of the tooting motif, if you try you can hear the toddler through the piano clusters, obstinately honking a horn in a spirit of malicious fun. The B-section soothingly—and, on another level, logically—tries to detract from the tooting, but 'Toot' will not be outdone. He comes back strong in the third A-section. The tune is taken at medium tempo. In his solo Monk works humorous contrasts on the thematic material. He is so forceful that Max Roach takes up the rhythmic surface structure, an approach more commonly associated with Art Blakey.

'Sweet and Lovely', the standard that sounds like what it's called, undergoes a sweet-and-sour reconfiguration at Monk's hands. Max Roach ratchets it up to double time. Again and again a cheeky reminiscence of 'Tea for Two' can be heard in the piano's left hand. 'Bye-Ya' is a hammering Afro-Cuban song by Monk. The interpretation sticks to the Afro-Cuban groove, highlighting it with thick chords.

The rhythmically and harmonically complex song 'Monk's Dream' is played in medium-fast tempo. In the presentation of the theme the implications of odd meter are brought out in the bass and drums. The tune sounds as if it were a 'frozen Monk improvisation.' Monk's solo is rich in modulations. One can make out a continuously flowing line, such as one might expect to hear ten years later from Eric Dolphy. 'Trinkle Tinkle' is a thematicized 'piano-strum' in medium-fast tempo, with increasingly fast sixteenth note triplets in the treble that alternate with regular sixteenth notes. With the superimposed song form, the piece has a decidedly comic effect, heightened by the percussive figures hammered out on the piano. In his accompaniment and breaks Max Roach helps to bring this aspect out.

On 'These Foolish Things' the untuned piano is used to good effect, to highlight the theme of the piece.

MONK
Prestige LP-7053; CD OJC 016

Julius Watkins (fr h), Sonny Rollins (ts), Monk (p), Percy Heath (b), Willie Jones (d); November 13, 1953:
LET'S CALL THIS / THINK OF ONE (2 takes)
Ray Copeland (tp), Frank Foster (ts), Monk (p), Curley Russell (b), Art Blakey (d); May 10 or 11, 1954:
WE SEE / SMOKE GETS IN YOUR EYES / LOCOMOTIVE / HACKENSACK

This Prestige LP also brings together material from two different recording dates. Rudy Van Gelder saw to it that the sound was excellent, something evident on the very first piece. Monk's 'We

See' is in song form, and taken mildly up-tempo. It is arranged for horns. Monk has the first solo and plays in a very relaxed style. Art Blakey creates some unusual and effective sound effects. Frank Foster's direct and unpretentious contribution on the sax sounds refreshing from today's perspective, when the few saxophonists who don't sound like Coltrane imitate Sonny Rollins. Ray Copeland was Monk's favorite trumpeter. He impresses us here with his singing tone and his sympathy with Monk's music as much as with his flashy high notes. 'Smoke Gets in Your Eyes' is another standard that Monk frequently liked to 'recompose' on solo piano. Here horns and a rhythm section are on hand, but restricted to supporting roles.

The remaining numbers on the disc are all Monk originals. 'Locomotive' is a gem. It is a cunning and exquisite musical portrait of a steam locomotive written in song form, whose A-section consists of only four bars, while the bridge has the usual eight. The piano and trumpet furnish the equivalents in sound of the train's wheel and eccentric rod movements. The saxophone mimics the sound of belching steam. It ascends to a higher register in the B-section, as we imagine the engine speeding up. The locomotive finally attains cruising speed in the third A-section. In his solo Monk interprets the mechanical sound of the theme in a softer and more melodic manner. Ray Copeland's trumpet solo eventually clears up the steam, and so the listener is left standing alongside Monk, the ingenious engineer, enjoying a view of the landscape as it slowly and smoothly glides by. The sax sends puffy clouds aloft, while Blakey from time to time energizes the steam system with hissing sounds. Before bringing the train to a stop, engineer Monk gives a demonstration of his own and the engine's dexterity, and the vehicle responds with the most evenly punctuated sounds of the number. As the reader may have guessed, this writer loves trains and is particularly fond of this artful miniature.

A sly portrait of a different kind is represented by 'Hackensack.'

The title refers to the town in New Jersey where Rudy Van Gelder's studio was located, and is dedicated to the engineer. In the plan of the A-section the melody resembles a more refined, abbreviated version of 'Well, You Needn't.' In the presentation of the theme the horns are in shrill contrast to the piano. Over the taut tempo Monk plays in rather a blowing-style. Frank Foster is the first soloist. Monk's accompaniment lets him go his own way, and we are soon reminded of Foster's robust qualities as a swing artist. In concert with Blakey, on the other hand, Monk pulls Copeland, in his solo, definitely in the direction of his own style. Copeland acquits himself bravely, and is soon succeeded by an earthy yet melodic drum solo, which leads logically to the reprise.

'Let's Call This' was recorded on Friday the 13th of November, 1953. There were unforeseen difficulties with the date. Julius Watkins had to substitute for the ailing Ray Copeland on short notice. And because Monk and Rollins, who had the music with them, were held up in traffic on the way to the studio and arrived two hours late, Watkins was left with little time to prepare for the recordings. The medium-fast song theme 'Let's Call This' sounds as if it were a pop song that suddenly strayed into bebop territory. In Sonny Rollins' solo one senses that he has studied and absorbed Monk's ideas, though he tries to maintain his own individuality. The French horn—a curiosity in jazz—comes through the changes without embarrassing itself. Monk's solo is solid, but nothing special. 'Think of One' is taken in the same tempo. It is an AABA theme developed from a fanfare-like motif. Monk plays a compelling solo, which is matched by Rollins' contribution. Watkins is more with it here, and gets to play longer. A piano solo composed of chord clusters leads back to the theme. On the second take the ensemble passages are better, but the solos are less compelling. Willie Jones keeps good time on the drums, but plays without any imaginative flair. The sound quality falls short of Rudy Van Gelder's standards.

It is not without a certain irony, that on this 'unlucky day', the only piece that would succeed happens to bear the ill-starred date in its title. It will be discussed with the next record.

Thelonious Monk / Sonny Rollins
Prestige LP 7075; CD: OJC 059

Julius Watkins (fr h), Sonny Rollins (ts), Monk (p), Percy Heath (b), Willie Jones (d); November 13, 1953:
FRIDAY THE THIRTEENTH
Monk (p), Percy Heath (b), Art Blakey (d); September 22, 1954:
WORK / NUTTY
Sonny Rollins (ts), Monk (p), Tommy Potter (b), Art Taylor (d); October 25, 1954:
THE WAY YOU LOOK TONIGHT / I WANT TO BE HAPPY

This album combines material from the performance dates documented on the two previous records, together with material from a later session, on which Sonny Rollins served as leader, and Rudy Van Gelder was the engineer. The two numbers from this later date are standards, rather than Monk compositions as on the remainder of the disc. The disc opens with the standards. 'The Way You Look Tonight' is introduced by Rollins up-tempo. He shapes his solo in the forceful, swinging style he is known for, and Monk offers supportive accompaniment. In his piano solo he restricts himself to a brief but not untypical contribution. Rollins has something more to express prior to the reprise. 'I Want to be Happy' follows a similar pattern, but Monk's solo here is stronger. The disk unfortunately does not include 'More Than You Know' from the October 25, 1954 session. This take can be heard on *Sonny Rollins, Movin' Out* (Prestige LP 7058). It is handled by the band in typical fashion. The tune was originally a popular song, and one of those relatively fast ballads that Monk liked. It is difficult to imagine anyone who could interpret this kind of music better than Rollins with his sardonic sense of humor.

'Work' is another one of the 1954 trio recordings on this album. It is a typical piano-driven, fast AABA theme with whirling figures in the treble set off by dark figures in the bass. These elements are elaborated in the piano solo. Blakey plays an interesting solo, in the first part of which he persistently accompanies himself on the ride cymbal. A short and concise bass solo leads to a final piano solo, leading to the reprise in a paraphrased form.

In 'Nutty' the treble figures are replaced by chord clusters, and the AABA form is given a blues coloring. After the brief piano solo the bass and piano engage in a dialogue, in which Monk for his part is very laconic. Blakey drums a long and eloquent solo back to the reprise.

'Friday the Thirteenth' is Monk's riff-style composition and commentary on the recording situation of that particular day. A four bar motif is four times pushed through a falling cadence in medium-fast tempo. The slightly sorrowful melody moves all the participants to comment in a uniformly morose manner. This leads, after Monk's solo, to a four-bar interchange among the horns. Monk summarizes the ideas before the recapitulation. This is certainly the most successful take of this Friday date.

Portrait of an Ermite
Swing M 33342
later as **The Prophet** (Vogue 500-104); reissued on CD as
Solo 1954 (Vogue 111502)
Monk (p); June 7, 1954:
MANGANESE / SMOKE GETS IN YOUR EYES / PORTRAIT
OF AN ERMITE / OFF MINOR / ERONEL / 'ROUND MID-
NIGHT / REFLECTIONS / WELL, YOU NEEDN'T /
HACKENSACK

It was almost certainly the scarcity of adequate sidemen living in Paris in 1954, rather than a deliberate production decision, that led Monk to make his first solo album. In any case the French specialist label Swing (later Vogue) gave him the opportunity to interpret pieces of his own choosing in a relaxed atmosphere, just him and his piano. He reverted to material that he had already handled for Prestige and Blue Note. But in the absence of horn arrangements, and by virtue of Monk's spare, almost crude piano style, these pieces sound like they have been distilled to their logical essence. Many sound clumsy and even bizarre; Monk was later to make more virtuosic solo recordings. And yet, despite their sketchy character, these interpretations achieve a level of definitiveness, thanks in large part to the pervasive beat, marked evenly but never slavishly by the left hand. This gives "Round Midnight' in particular a strange, fascinating beauty.

The list of numbers on the original cover is misleading (not to mention the misspelling of 'eremite' in the title). 'Manganese' is actually 'We See', 'Portrait of an Ermite' is 'Reflections', and the piece identified as 'Reflections' should be 'Evidence.' Moreover, a version of 'Hackensack' was recorded that was filed under the title 'Well, You Needn't (Take 2)'; it was omitted from the original 9¾-inch LP for lack of space.

With its unpolished angularity, and its interpretations focused solely on the essentials of the melody, this recording represents

Monk at his best when taken 'straight, no chaser': pure and undiluted.

Miles Davis and the Modern Jazz Giants
Prestige LP 7150; CD: OJC 347

PRESTIGE 7150
MILES DAVIS AND THE MODERN JAZZ GIANTS
MILT JACKSON/THELONIOUS MONK/PERCY HEATH/KENNY CLARKE
JOHN COLTRANE/RED GARLAND/PAUL CHAMBERS/PHILLY JOE JONES

Miles Davis (tp), Milt Jackson (vib), Monk (p), Percy Heath (b), Kenny Clarke (d); December 24, 1954:
BAGS' GROOVE (2 takes) / BEMSHA SWING / SWING SPRING / THE MAN I LOVE (2 takes)

The initial takes of both 'Bags' Groove' and 'The Man I Love' have already been described at length in the first section of the book. The second takes correspond to the first in the sequence and character of the solos, but in both cases are less focused and forceful. 'Bemsha Swing' consists of one four-bar phrase which resembles the 'Bags' Groove' motif, aligned with a set chord pattern. The pattern consists of four bars each: AA on the tonic, B on the subdominant, and A on the tonic again. This structure approximates to the first two-thirds of a blues progression, and with its affinity to the blues scale the tune overall impresses one as a continuous blues movement which never comes full circle. Monk plays the four-bar riff motif as an intro before the whole theme is executed in unison by the front line. Nothing could prevent Monk from doing what he wanted to do on his own composition, and so he plays during Miles Davis' solo. The trumpeter is actually stimulated by Monk's vertical accents to some highly dramatic rhetoric in his horizontal explorations. Milt Jackson's playing is somewhat more coarse than on 'Bags' Groove', and Monk's additions are not quite as refined as before. In his solo he subjects the theme materials to droll blues reharmonizations. Davis' solo is prelude to an exchange with Milt Jackson, in which the pair trade four-bar phrases.

Miles Davis' 'Swing Spring' is a scale-derived AABA theme in accelerated tempo. The unison instrumentation of the A-section does not completely suit the elegance of the melodic line. But the trumpet solo is a delight, with a wealth of ideas. The piano sits out while bass and drums accompany Davis with great sympathy and light-footed agility. Milt Jackson is no less inventive in his turn, and Monk accompanies him with abstractly beautiful and well-placed tonal jabs. Davis takes an additional solo while the piano lays out. Now it's Monk's turn, and he demonstrates that his sententious style could accommodate itself to the dominant musical flow. There is an encore from Milt Jackson. The melody, heard again in the reprise, seems much more powerful and pungent now than at the start of the number. It puts the finishing touch on a collection that documents one of the most divine moments in jazz.

This record also includes some numbers by Davis' mid-fifties quintet with John Coltrane.

The Riverside Years

Thelonious Monk Plays Duke Ellington
Riverside RLP 12-201; CD: OJC 024

Monk (p), Oscar Pettiford (b), Kenny Clarke (d); July 21 and 27, 1955:
MOOD INDIGO / IT DON'T MEAN A THING IF IT AIN'T GOT THAT SWING / SOPHISTICATED LADY / I GOT IT BAD / I LET A SONG GO OUT OF MY HEART / CARAVAN / BLACK AND TAN FANTASY / SOLITUDE (p solo)

With this trio performance Monk's recording career with Riverside began. The Ellington interpretations were the idea of producer Orrin Keepnews, and were intended to serve a 'pedagogical' purpose (see above, page 59). He later maintained that Monk would never have consented to go along with something he didn't want to do himself. In the liner notes Keepnews also reports, however, that Monk had to learn some of the tunes from a collection of Ellington sheet-music. So this record can in no sense be regarded as a labor of love.

The selection of titles is limited to popular, structurally conventional Ellington songs. Monk's general approach is to vary the theme rather than explore bold harmonies. He gives generous solo time to Oscar Pettiford, the bass pioneer and sometime member of the Ellington orchestra. Pettiford's supple solos consistently hew to the theme. Kenny Clarke's role is limited to discreet brush work. The somewhat monotonous moderately fast tempos highlight the conservative nature of the disk. Only 'Caravan' is rhythmically more adventurous. Pettiford's contribution here is more exciting than the leader's. It is interesting to compare this piece with Ellington's own excursion into the modern, Monk world of jazz, on his album *Money Jungle*. Duke's interpretation of 'Caravan' there is actually more daring and Monkish.

When purchasing *Thelonious Monk Plays Duke Ellington* one should take care to avoid editions engineered with an artificial stereo sound, which gives Monk's piano an additional echo around the edges. One is better served by the Milestone double album *The Riverside Trios* (Milestone 47052), which also contains the Riverside album *The Unique Thelonious Monk.*

Gigi Gryce
Nica's Tempo
Signal S 1201; Savoy MG 12137; CD: Savoy SV-0216

Gigi Gryce (as), Monk (p), Percy Heath (b), Art Blakey (d); October 15, 1955:
BRAKE'S SAKE / GALLOP'S GALLOP / SHUFFLE BOIL / NICA'S TEMPO
Gigi Gryce (as), Art Farmer (tp), Jimmy Cleveland (tb), Danny Bank (bs), Gunther Schuller (fr h), Bill Barber (tuba), Horace Silver (p), Oscar Pettiford (b), Kenny Clarke (d); October 22, 1955:
SPECULATION / IN A MEDITATING MOOD / SMOKE SIGNAL / KERRY DANCE
Gigi Gryce (as), Art Farmer (tp), Eddie Bert (tb), Cecil Payne (bs), Julius Watkins (fr h), Bill Barber (tuba), Horace Silver (p), Oscar Pettiford (b), Art Blakey (d), Ernestine Anderson (voc); October 22, 1955:
SOCIAL CALL / (YOU'LL ALWAYS BE) THE ONE I LOVE

The mere fact that the first three pieces named are debut performances of Monk compositions makes this a kind of unofficial Monk album. On 'Shuffle Boil' a bass vamp leads to an obliquely ascending motif with a lagging bass line played simultaneously on bass and piano. In the bridge the motifs thicken to a continuous melodic line that stands in charming contrast to the angularity of the A-section. Gigi Gryce plays a solo which, with its gliding ease, owes as much to Charlie Parker as to Lee Konitz. This ethereal quality carries over into Monk's solo. Before the reprise Blakey trades four-bar solos with Gigi Gryce, and the light-footed and subtle character of Blakey's fours are uncharacteristic. 'Brake's Sake' is a fanfare-like melody with magnificently displaced rhythms. The solos by Gryce and Monk are again wonderfully relaxed. 'Gallop's Gallop' represents something like the translation of the motif technique of 'Brake's Sake' into Monk's unwieldy but logical linearity. Gryce and Monk's solos are again relaxed. If the Monk tunes were not performed in his favorite floating bounce tempo, the gracefulness that characterizes these recordings would be lost. This becomes clear on 'Nica's Tempo', the only Gryce original here. The handling of the thematic shorthand motifs is much more catchy. After buoyant solos by Gryce and Monk, Gryce and Blakey play fours, leading to a classic Blakey solo. The reprise brings to a close one of the most beautiful Monk albums, which strictly speaking is not a Monk album at all.

The Unique Thelonious Monk
Riverside RLP 12-209; CD: OJC 064

Monk (p), Oscar Pettiford (b), Art Blakey (d); March 17, 1956:
LIZA /YOU ARE TOO BEAUTIFUL /JUST YOU JUST ME /
MEMORIES OF YOU (p solo)
Same personnel; April 3, 1956:
HONEYSUCKLE ROSE / DARN THAT DREAM / TEA FOR
TWO

Monk's second Riverside album is also devoted to the interpretation of other people's compositions. It is not, however, restricted to the works of one composer, but covers a range of standards. They appear to be more familiar to Monk, and it is evident that he was more involved with their actual selection. 'Liza' is taken up-tempo. Blakey pushes discreetly behind Monk's spacious solo, then ventures on what is for him a very concise and disciplined solo. The theme sounds almost as if it were being satirized in the periphrastic reprise. 'Memories of You' is performed with rubato and presented as a melancholy mood piece. After the theme the beat is then toyed with in Monk's left hand. In contrast to this almost tender interpretation stands the down and dissonant 'Honeysuckle Rose', taken in jumping stride rhythm. Monk gives little of himself in his first solo, relying more on the bass, which then plays a subtly exciting solo. The second time around he is more outgoing. Blakey's brightly humorous solo stimulates Monk to a transitional digression, before the theme is reprised in a form slightly altered from before.

'Darn that Dream' is a ballad that was often interpreted by Billie Holiday, Monk's idol among female vocalists. Like her, Monk elevates the melody above the level of kitsch by the displacement of phrases, turning it into a genuinely moving piece. Oscar Pettiford constructs a beautiful bass solo from variations on the theme. He never abandons the instrument's low register for the sake of the high note virtuosity popular today. 'Tea for Two' is introduced rubato with a quick-moving bass line that creates a feeling of *déjà vu*, then becomes a 'walk' delivered pizzicato. The treatment of the melody is at once cheeky and respectful, as on 'Honeysuckle Rose', except that a waltz parody replaces the jump overtones. 'You Are Too Beautiful' is performed as a ballad but without sentimentality. In the opening melody there is a pretty section where the piano and bass play in unison. The bass has the only solo and acquits itself in bravura fashion, with free, ambitious phrasing. 'Just You Just Me' is an oft-played jazz standard. Of all the melodies here it is the one most suited to serve as a blowing vehicle for all three musicians.

Although it consists of covers, 'The Unique' offers absolutely authentic Monk music, and sounds a good deal fresher than the otherwise similar *Plays Ellington.* The sound is up to Rudy Van Gelder's usual high standards.

Brilliant Corners
Riverside RLP 12-226; OJC 026-2

Ernie Henry (as), Sonny Rollins (ts), Monk (p and celeste), Max Roach (d) Oscar Pettiford (b); October 9, 1956:

BA-LUE BOLIVAR BA-LUES-ARE / PANNONICA
Same personnel; October 15, 1956:
BRILLIANT CORNERS
*Clark Terry (tp), Sonny Rollins (ts), Monk (p), Paul Chambers (b),
Max Roach (d, tympani); December 7, 1956:*
BEMSHA SWING / I SURRENDER DEAR (p solo)

With *Brilliant Corners*, Riverside thought it was time for an album on which Monk played his own compositions primarily. They did not skimp on sidemen; in putting the quartet together only musicians of the first order were considered. Monk himself knew what this opportunity meant and produced three new pieces for the occasion. They sound perfectly natural at first hearing; closer listening, however, reveals their technical sophistication, not to mention their inner wit and power.

The 'brilliant corners' that Monk leads the musicians around on the title track are very steeply pitched. In a condensed and irregular ABA′ scheme, in which A consists of eight bars, but B and A′ are seven bars each, the accents of the melody come at different, unexpected places with every new motif. And yet the whole thing seems natural rather than contrived. After the theme is run through once, it is repeated in double time. The alternation between slow and fast tempi is reproduced in the parade of solos. In exploring the difficult form Sonny Rollins is accompanied by Monk with a mixture of support and provocation, resulting in a glorious statement that works masterful variations on the theme. During Monk's solo the bassist betrays a slight uncertainty. Owing to such lapses a quarrel ensued between Monk and Pettiford. They never worked together again.

In Monk's playing the harmonic beauty of this composition is illuminated by the contrast between the discreet playing of the bass notes and the elaboration of the melodic motifs in the right hand. Ernie Henry's solo, without piano accompaniment, is extremely eloquent. Unfortunately this musician died a year after the recording. Max Roach offers a masterly example of melodic solo drumming before the reprise.

The onomatopoetically entitled 'Ba-Lue Bolivar Ba-lues-are' is a compositional master stroke. The typical four-bar blues motif opens with a movement suggesting three over four, which following its repetition turns into a genuine three movement with a B-section quality. Ernie Henry plays a splendid modern blues solo. Monk's contribution is spare, heavily reliant on the bass, and full of fresh ideas, which in later performances increasingly recur as 'Monk clichés.' Rollins' solo is somewhat pedestrian, but Monk's spacious accompaniment is very fine, amounting almost to a duet. Finally, Pettiford makes his bass tell a blues story. Then Max Roach, who has accompanied everyone with exceptional taste to this point, plays an equally tasteful solo before the recapitulation. 'Pannonica' is Monk's delicate tribute in ballad form, free of false sentiment, to Pannonica de Koenigswarter. In the studio he came upon a celeste, an instrument similar to a glockenspiel but with a piano-style keyboard. He positioned it alongside the piano in order to play both simultaneously. In his hands this 'angelic instrument' produces a bright, hard tone. Rollins interprets the theme more than adequately while the brushes keep double-time. He remains anchored to the theme presented on piano. During his solo Monk's right hand plays subtle thematic variations on the celeste, while the left contributes darkly glowing and serene chords.

Monk's unaccompanied solo on 'I Surrender Dear' extends the mood of 'Pannonica.' On 'Bemsha Swing' Clark Terry takes the place of Ernie Henry, who had left Monk's band for Dizzy Gillespie's orchestra. Paul Chambers substitutes for Oscar Pettiford, who had been sacked. This time it was Max Roach's turn to make a discovery in the studio. He supplemented his kit with tympani, giving the rather simple theme a powerful allure. During Rollins' solo he makes the tympani thunder. Unaccompanied by piano, Rollins in his solo translates this percussive power into his own playing. Clark Terry, on the other hand, seems overwhelmed by the piano and enhanced percussion. Monk himself keeps it short. Max Roach gets somewhat lost in tympani effects during his solo. Paul Chambers' workmanlike contribution on bass is refreshing by comparison. A brief saxophone solo leads to the reprise.

Brilliant Corners is one of the most significant Monk records. The three originals, recently penned and each a high point of Monk's compositional *oeuvre*, adapt well to the quintet setting. With this record Monk finally achieved his breakthrough. Another reason for its success is that it was conceived as an organic whole; the unaccompanied piano solo 'I Surrender Dear' is no exception in this regard. So it is puzzling that Orrin Keepnews chose to omit it from the double album reissue *Brilliance* (Milestone M-47023) in favor of a version of 'Played Twice' that had in turn been left off *Five by Monk by Five*, the other LP reissued with this twofer. In any case, the performance can be found on the Milestone solo sampler, *Pure Monk* (M-47004).

Thelonious Himself
Riverside RLP 12-235; CD: OJC 254

Monk (p solo); April 5, 1957:
GHOST OF A CHANCE / I SHOULD CARE / 'ROUND MID-
NIGHT
Monk (p solo); April 12 and 16, 1957:
APRIL IN PARIS / ALL ALONE / I'M GETTING SENTIMEN-
TAL OVER YOU / FUNCTIONAL / MONK'S MOOD (with John
Coltrane (ts), Wilbur Ware (b))

After the success of *Brilliant Corners*, Riverside conceived the idea
of recording an 'American' solo album with Monk. The title is apt
insofar as it captures the prevailing mood: Monk sounds as if he
were at home, by himself, in front of his piano. In relaxed tempi,
often with rubato, standards are subjected to a benign and leisurely exploration. Whoever expects to find here the definitive
quality of the French solo performances of 1954 will be disap-
pointed, however. An exception is Monk's own blues 'Functional.'
It too begins in a very relaxed style. But by virtue of the pervasive
beat and the healthy infusion of stride piano (derived from James
P. Johnson), it achieves a compelling density.

The second Monk original on the record, "Round Midnight',
is interpreted rubato, like the standards. The slow-motion interpretation permits the listener to follow Monk's thought processes
step-by-step. But the original 1954 interpretation is more forceful.
The third and final Monk composition here, 'Monk's Mood', goes
beyond the solo format, in a way, though it is not a real trio recording, and not a duet either; the presence of sax and bass just
adds tonal color to Monk's solo exploration. Monk first plays solo
through the whole form, in a rhapsodic, rubato style. After a passionate intro by Coltrane, he and Monk go through the form again
as a close-knit unit, Coltrane adding only slight embellishments
to the melody. For the last couple of bars they are joined by the
bass. All the pieces through 'Monk's Mood' are also available on
Pure Monk (Milestone M-47004).

Sonny Rollins Volume 2
Blue Note BLP 1558; CD: Blue Note B21Y-81558-2

Jay Jay Johnson (tb), Sonny Rollins (ts), Horace Silver (p), Paul Chambers (b), Art Blakey (d); April 14, 1957:
WHY DON'T I / WAIL MARCH / YOU STEPPED OUT OF A DREAM / POOR BUTTERFLY
Jay Jay Johnson (tb), Sonny Rollins (ts), Horace Silver (p), Monk (p), Paul Chambers (b), Art Blakey (d); April 14, 1957:
MISTERIOSO
Sonny Rollins (ts), Monk (p), Paul Chambers (b), Art Blakey (d); April 14, 1957:
REFLECTIONS

Although not an album on which Monk is leader, *Sonny Rollins Volume 2* belongs in a complete Monk collection. The two numbers Monk plays on are among his best performances with horns. That he was willing to enter the studio as a sideman with his old label can only be construed as a mark of his respect for Sonny Rollins. The numbers without Monk are fine, carefully produced Blue Note blowing sessions. The ingenious and vigorous bass of Paul Chambers lays down a rock-solid foundation, to which Art Blakey's muscular and sonorous fireworks are anchored. While playing with Monk on Monk compositions, Rollins was always faithful to the spirit of the composer. In this respect 'Misterioso' (now in Monk's preferred spelling with an 'i') is especially interesting. Monk accompanies Rollins, in the course of which the saxophonist sounds more earthy and bluesy than Milt Jackson on the debut performance of the piece. Monk gets into the spirit of the saxophonist in his own less abstract, more powerful solo. Jay Jay Johnson is accompanied by Horace Silver; now the piece becomes an elegant, swinging, modern blues, with restrained, supportive piano. Silver's solo preserves the mood. Paul Chambers disrupts it with an uncommonly powerful solo. After a horn/drum exchange Monk, in especially angular mode, anticipates the re-prise, that then follows in a chorus by the horns.

Sonny Rollins shows himself a masterful and sensitive inter-preter of the Monk ballad 'Reflections.' He is able to paraphrase the melody in his own distinctive way while remaining true to the spirit of the work. Monk plays a beautiful, detailed solo that com-ports especially well with the rhythmic interplay of Blakey and Chambers. Rollins spins the thread further in his contribution, and the reprise brings the proceedings to a logical close. Two very distinctive musical personalities prove ideal partners. Rudy Van Gelder's engineering is up to his usually high standards.

Art Blakey's Jazz Messengers with Thelonious Monk
Atlantic SD 1278; CD: Atlantic 781332-2

Bill Hardman (tp), Johnny Griffin (ts), Monk (p), Spanky DeBrest (b), Art Blakey (d); May 14, 1957:
BLUE MONK / I MEAN YOU
Same personnel; May 15, 1957:
RHYTHM-A-NING / PURPLE SHADES / EVIDENCE / IN WALKED BUD

When the international label Atlantic brought Art Blakey into the studio they engaged Monk as the pianist. But Monk is more than a sideman here. Except for 'Purple Shades', Johnny Griffin's me-dium-fast traditional blues, all the numbers are Monk originals. He is chief soloist on the album as well. If the result is not a genu-ine Monk album, the reason is only that, aside from Blakey him-self, the 'Jazz Messengers' were not entirely comfortable with Monk's music. This goes especially for Bill Hardmann and Spanky DeBrest. DeBrest belongs to that species of bebop bassist who can be relied on to make the bass 'walk', but without much elegance, ingenuity, or subtle swing. And so Art Blakey does not sound as cogent or inspired as when he played with Oscar Pettiford or Paul Chambers. On 'Evidence' trumpeter Bill Hardman puts up a good show, yet it is a cause for regret that the interplay with Monk is not more daring and intense, because Hardman's sharp, biting tone and style of phrasing actually suit Monk quite well. Monk in his solo breaks up the harmonic implications of the melody into abrupt chords. The élan with which Johnny Griffin attacks his solo obviously provokes Monk, who actually sounds more inspired in his accompaniment than in his solo. Art Blakey's solo is adequate, but conventional Blakey.

'In Walked Bud' is taken somewhat more slowly than on the first performance. Griffin has the first solo and embarks on lively and good-humored play in double time. As on 'Evidence', there are intimations of his later work with Monk. The composer then plays odd motivic variations with great feeling for space and time. After this warm-up Bill Hardman is more inspired and to the point. The best piece on the album is 'Blue Monk.' All the participants are naturally at home in the blues idiom, and the fact that the melody is presented in a smart and witty arrangement takes care of the rest (even the bassist is trusted with a solo). Monk's contribution is darkly gleaming in a bluesy sort of way, and yet devoid of blues clichés.

On 'I Mean You' Johnny Griffin again has the first solo while Monk lays out. His own solo consequently gives the impression of being well planned. Bill Hardman, at the urging of Monk and Blakey, is emboldened to venture into Monk-like corners, and with good results. Blakey plays an enjoyably relaxed solo, before the reprise comes around. The number that best succeeds in capturing Monk's spirit, however, is 'Rhythm-a-ning', the piece that, in Monk's own phrase, 'swings by itself.' Monk introduces it and plays the first solo in close collaboration with Blakey, who comments on and anticipates Monk's fragments of chords and melody.

Bill Hardman finally gets with it and relates completely to Monk's dense and disturbing accompaniment. He becomes an ideal interpreter of Monk's sound, with the result that the composer accompanies him with obvious pleasure. Griffin makes an obvious (and largely successful) effort to lift the proceedings to a new level, and Blakey then plays one of his best solos before drumming eloquently in the reprise. This 'Rhythm-a-ning' is more compact, coherent, and compelling than the first performance. With Johnny Griffin's traditional blues the disc concludes in a relaxed fashion. The solos are not so Monk-inspired as on 'Blue Monk', and on this account a shade looser. It is odd, that after the confident and relaxed performances on these two numbers, the last pair from the same recording date, 'Evidence' and 'In Walked Bud', come off somewhat flat and inhibited.

Monk's Music
Riverside RLP 12-242; CD: OJC 084

Ray Copeland (tp), Gigi Gryce (as), John Coltrane (ts), Coleman Hawkins (ts), Wilbur Ware (b), Art Blakey (d); June 26, 1957:
WELL, YOU NEEDN'T / OFF MINOR / EPISTROPHY / EPISTROPHY (alternate take) / CREPUSCULE WITH NELLIE / ABIDE WITH ME / RUBY, MY DEAR
CD bonus tracks: OFF MINOR (take 4) / CREPUSCULE WITH NELLIE (takes 4 and 5)

Whether *Monk's Music* is the appropriate title for this all-star offering is open to doubt. Although the horn players strive to do right by Monk's compositions, it is clear that Coleman Hawkins and Gigi Gryce often fail to adapt to his world of sound. John Coltrane, whose work with Monk was only beginning at the time of this recording, plays in rather a timid and reserved fashion, which must be due in part to the imposing presence of Hawkins, the 'father of the tenor saxophone.' Moreover, on the extended pieces 'Well, You Needn't' and 'Epistrophy' there is no real ensemble playing; instead they are treated as blowing sessions 'by and with Monk.'

After a fifty-one second musical gag, consisting of a chorale by Monk's nineteenth-century British namesake William Henry Monk, and performed by the horns, the first Monk number, 'Well, You Needn't', begins. The arrangement is promising, and Monk's solo is engaging, but the beat of the rhythm section is singularly flat. The sound of the bass is weak, and Wilbur Ware rarely achieved the imaginative heights of Percy Heath, Oscar Pettiford, or Paul Chambers. Art Blakey's drumming is also far less exciting than when he played with those masters. Coltrane plays without much bite, Ray Copeland at least displays more assurance, the bass walks in its solo more than it develops ideas, Blakey's solo is almost too energetic. He is followed by Coleman Hawkins who cannot sustain the same energy level. Monk tries to come to his old mate's rescue, prodding him with contrasting chords. The old champ finally regains his confidence and comes off with his dignity intact. But not even the most supportive comping by Monk can free Gigi Gryce's alto playing from its bebop clichés and its chirping sound. In the piano introduction to the reprise things get back on track, but the take remains a disappointment.

'Ruby, My Dear' is presented by Hawkins. The other horn players lay out. The old master's ballad interpretation meets the sound of this Monk song with majestic tone and serenity. He also has all the time he needs to develop his ideas. The composer restricts himself on his solo to a brief transition to the reprise.

In 'Off Minor' the septet is effectively deployed in the opening presentation of the theme. Hawkins has the first solo and makes his way through the form with ease. Behind him and trumpeter Ray Copeland Monk's accompaniment is deft and authoritative. His own solo makes considerable use of space–the kind Miles Davis once compared to doors thrust open to afford deep perspectives on the music. Before the drum break Wilbur Ware contributes a brief but eloquent solo. The reprise brings to an end the most compact track on the record.

On 'Epistrophy' the head arrangement is again effective. Coltrane has the first solo. It is more passionate than his contribution on 'Well, You Needn't', and well-structured. Monk lays out during Ray Copeland's solo. He starts tentatively but grows more self-confident. Gigi Gryce also has to manage without piano; Art Blakey instead supports him with busy accents, trying to add color to the rather pallid alto sax. Ware plays a solo based on walking lines. Then there is a moment of uncertainty among Monk, Hawkins, and Blakey as to who should go next. Blakey finally asserts himself, but during his supercharged solo Hawkins makes a vain attempt to enter. When it really is his turn, he makes an uninhibited statement, which does not wander too far from the theme, however. Then it is Monk's turn; before everybody joins in the recapitulation, his right hand hammers out funky chromatic figures.

'Crepuscule with Nellie', Monk's hymn to his wife, is first stated by piano, bass, and drums alone. As always when Monk played this tune, there are no solos over the highly personal theme. The horn players then come in for a richly harmonized reprise. I personally feel that the usually brilliant Rudy Van Gelder could have captured the ensemble, particularly the bass, in a more full-bodied way, on this, Monk's first stereo album for Riverside.

Thelonious Monk with John Coltrane
Jazzland JLP-46; CD: OJC 039

Monk (p solo); April 12, 1957:
FUNCTIONAL (alternate take)
Ray Copeland (tp), Gigi Gryce (as), Coleman Hawkins (ts), John Coltrane (ts), Monk (p), Wilbur Ware (b), Art Blakey (d); June 26, 1957:
EPISTROPHY (fragment) / OFF MINOR (take 4)
John Coltrane (ts), Monk (p), Wilbur Ware (b), Shadow Wilson (d); July 1957:
NUTTY / RUBY, MY DEAR / TRINKLE TINKLE

This curious compilation was first released in 1961. The exact recording dates of the three quartet recordings are uncertain. The producer Orrin Keepnews made contradictory statements, assigning them to July 1957 as well as 'early 1958.' On the quartet numbers, in any case, Monk and Coltrane make outstanding collaborators. The sound engineering on the monaural quartet recordings is far superior to the septet recordings in stereo. Wilbur Ware's bass playing may be charitably described as competent, but hardly virtuosic. Coltrane's playing on 'Ruby, My Dear' sounds more genuinely Monkish than Hawkins' interpretation on *Monk's Music.* Coltrane is the lone soloist, and he plays as if the piece were written by, or for, him. 'Trinkle Tinkle' has a melody line suggestive of running scales, making it ideal for Coltrane's famous scale-oriented approach. Thus in his solo he can process the thematic materials with his 'sheets of sound', producing something completely new and personal. Clearly stimulated by Coltrane's solo, Monk's contribution is equally beautiful and concise. The bassist follows, then the reprise, composed of precise unison playing between the piano and sax, relieved by sharp drum breaks.

The performance of 'Off Minor' does not greatly differ from that on *Monk's Music*. 'Nutty' is the third quartet recording. Coltrane again plays without holding back. Monk gives him his head and sits out. In his solo he plays with the thematic elements in good humor. With the reprise, perhaps the best performances of a Monk quartet conclude. The performance of 'Epistrophy' differs from the master on *Monk's Music* in that Hawkins does not take part in the soloing. 'Functional' is an interesting alternative performance from the *Thelonious Himself* recording date. And like the master, it represents superior solo Monk.

Mulligan Meets Monk
Riverside RLP 12-247; CD: OJC 301

Gerry Mulligan (bs), Monk (p), Wilbur Ware (b), Shadow Wilson (d); August 12, 1957:

STRAIGHT, NO CHASER / RHYTHM-A-NING / I MEAN
YOU
Same personnel; August 1957:
SWEET AND LOVELY / DECIDEDLY / 'ROUND MIDNIGHT

The critics were not much taken with this encounter between Monk
and the protagonist of white Cool Jazz. Its commercial success,
on the other hand, vindicated Orrin Keepnews, and even before
the album was delivered to stores Riverside got many advance
orders. The undeniable charm of the album derives from the fact
that both individuals remain true to themselves, and no half-
hearted jam session compromises are made. Mulligan deserves
credit for the grace with which he defers to the leadership of Monk,
ten years his senior. For his part, Monk is ready on 'Rhythm-a-
ning' to put up with a boldly simplified variation on the theme (in
the B-section especially) by Mulligan. The first piece on the album was recorded at the suggestion of Mulligan. He wanted to
perform this hymn to the witching hour with its composer. And
''Round Midnight' is actually the most cogent piece on the album. It is remarkable how Monk always managed to explore radi-
cally new territory when playing this, his most famous piece. On
'Rhythm-a-ning' Mulligan has some difficulty staying with Monk
in running through the changes, but Monk seems to take a certain
malicious pleasure in the fact; in any case, he plays much faster
and more fluently, in the bebop manner, than on his previous
recordings of the tune. Surprisingly, it is on the standard 'Sweet
and Lovely' that Mulligan and Monk seem most out of synch—so
strong is the latter's recomposition influence, both in the statement of the theme and during his accompaniment. In any case,
the piano solo is inspired.

'Decidedly' is Mulligan's contribution as a composer. In its
obvious dependence on the Charlie Shavers standard 'Undecided'
it betrays a certain imaginative poverty, not to say plagiarism.
Unencumbered by piano accompaniment Mulligan is free to de-

velop his continuous, effortlessly swinging lines. In his solo Monk impudently breaks up the theme material with caustic humor. Next, Wilbur Ware ventures to 'walk' unaccompanied. His sound is once again as dull and simple as on *Monk's Music.* On 'Straight, No Chaser' Mulligan handles the blues changes with consummate ease. Monk sits out during the saxophone solo. Mulligan, in turn, plays ground lines behind Monk's again rather fluent solo, which quotes from 'Salt Peanuts.' Ware in his solo plays daring double stop combinations, which involve plucking two or more strings on the bass at once, like a guitar.

On 'I Mean You' the soloists define themselves in contrast with one another, and as a result the bass comes off somewhat better. The rhythm section, anchored in Shadow Wilson's solidly swinging drumming, is generally an harmonically and tonally unifying force. During the A-section of the reprise there is a very interesting, lightly contrapuntal exchange between piano and sax. All the recordings of this disk with several alternate takes are collected on the Milestone twofer *Thelonious Monk and Gerry Mulligan – 'Round Midnight* (M-47067). Included is the nearly twenty-two minute long exploration of "Round Midnight' from the *Thelonious Himself* recording date, that preceded the master take that was released at the time. This master take forms the conclusion of the Milestone double album.

Clark Terry In Orbit
Riverside RLP 12-271; CD: OJC 302

Clark Terry (fl-h), Monk (p), Sam Jones (b), Philly Joe Jones (d); May 7 and 12, 1958:
IN ORBIT (GLOBETROTTER) / PEA-EYE (ZIP COED) / LET'S COOL ONE / ONE FOOT IN THE GUTTER / MOONLIGHT FIESTA / VERY NEAR BLUES / TRUST IN ME / ARGENTIA / BUCK'S BUSINESS
CD bonus track: FLUGELIN' THE BLUES

Actually this record does not belong in this context, for, in contrast to *Mulligan Meets Monk* and *Thelonious Monk and Art Blakey's*
Jazz Messengers, Monk is really only a sideman here and not the
leader. But it is precisely this circumstance that gives it a particular interest. In his career as an established musician Monk never
again effaced himself to this extent. He is clearly content–if always in his own style–to accommodate Clark Terry, and support
him in his elegantly nonchalant driving and swinging manner.
And there is only one number composed by the pianist. It is a
pleasure to listen to the pliant flow of ideas from the flugelhorn,
when deployed, as it is here, not as an exotic version of a trumpet,
but as an instrument in its own right–a novelty in jazz for the
time. With Sam Jones and Philly Joe Jones a rhythm section is at
work whose balanced mastery Monk himself seldom enjoyed in
his own bands at the time. The effect of Sam Jones' vigorous and
inventive playing is little diminished by the rather bass-unfriendly
recording technique. And thus the rhythmic foundation is of a
hip solidity, above which the flugelhorn and piano sound uncommonly fresh and alive.

Thelonious In Action
Riverside RLP 12-262; CD OJC 103

Misterioso
Riverside RLP 12-279; CD: OJC 206

Johnny Griffin (ts), Monk (p), Ahmen Abdul-Malik (b), Roy Haynes (d); July 9, 1958:
BLUES FIVE SPOT / IN WALKED BUD / EPISTROPHY (theme)
Same personnel; August 7, 1958:
BLUE MONK / EVIDENCE / EPISTROPHY / LIGHT BLUE / COMING ON THE HUDSON / RHYTHM-A-NING / NUTTY / BLUES FIVE SPOT / LET'S COOL ONE / IN WALKED BUD / JUST A GIGOLO (p solo) / MISTERIOSO

Blues Five Spot
Milestone M-912
Johnny Griffin (ts), Donald Byrd (t), Pepper Adams (bs), Monk (p), Wilbur Ware (b), Philly Joe Jones (d); February 25, 1958:
COMING ON THE HUDSON
Johnny Griffin (ts), Monk (p), Ahmed Abdul-Malik (b), Roy Haynes (d); July 9, 1958:
BLUES FIVE SPOT / [UNIDENTIFIED PIANO SOLO] / 'ROUND MIDNIGHT
Johnny Griffin (ts), Monk (p), Ahmed Abdul-Malik (b), Art Blakey (d); July 9, 1958:
BYE-YA / EPISTROPHY
Charlie Rouse (ts), Thad Jones (c), Monk (p), Sam Jones (b), Art Taylor (d); June 1959:
PLAYED TWICE

Charlie Rouse (ts), Monk (p), John Ore (b), Frankie Dunlop (d); April 18, 1961:
BODY AND SOUL (p solo) / CREPUSCULE WITH NELLIE

The sides on the first two records were recorded on July 9 and August 7, 1958, therefore at the end of Monk's first extended guest spot at the Five Spot; they are included unaltered on Milestone M-47043, *Thelonious Monk at the Five Spot. In Action* begins with 'Light Blue', a medium-fast, angular AA composition. The soloists are Griffin and Monk. The strengths of the album are immediately clear: Monk and Griffin perform outstandingly well together, in part because Griffin operates within Monk's parameters, and refrains from his eye-popping, high-speed acrobatics. Roy Haynes plays with that refined, multi-layered hipness that made him a model for Elvin Jones and Jack DeJohnette. Unfortunately the recording technique does not permit him to be appreciated adequately. The bass, for its part, is audible enough, but offers nothing but a reliable substructure.

'Coming on the Hudson' is a theme in AABA form, which, however, could hardly be less conventional. The A-section only has five bars, and the B-section consists of three-and-a-half. Add to this the fact that the rhythm of the entire melody is three against four. In mood and execution it has much in common with 'Light Blue.' In both cases Monk establishes a rather strict framework for the tenor solo with his dense comping. 'Rhythm-a-ning' is taken up-tempo. Johnny Griffin plays a long, hot solo, for the most part without comment from the piano. The wealth of ideas in Roy Haynes' accompaniment is a delight. Monk's contribution is more concentrated and spare than on the previous numbers, and fragmented in the manner of his playing with the Jazz Messengers. Abdul-Malik plays a sturdy, walking solo, which, however, grows increasingly shapeless. Roy Haynes drums a melodic solo full of counter-rhythms before the reprise. The tune of 'Epistrophy' is played as theme music only. 'Blue Monk' grooves nicely in medium tempo. Again, Monk lays out after the first couple of Griffin's choruses. Griffin then accelerates to double time. Roy Haynes, despite his lively and witty accents, keeps the tempo firmly anchored in the initial beat, but hints at double-time during Monk's solo. Abdul-Malik never deviates from solid four-to-the-bar walking, so the rhythmic pattern is never in doubt. After Monk's solo, the bass and drum solo in their turn, and their contributions are of the same interest as they were on 'Rhythm-a-ning.' This rigid solo sequence–tenor-piano-bass-drums–was to become a rather tiresome characteristic of the Monk quartet. 'Evidence', in somewhat accelerated time, likewise adheres to this sequence. Monk is again captured in good form. With 'Epistrophy' as theme music the record fades out.

Misterioso opens with 'Nutty.' Since bass and drums forego solos Monk is free to make a lengthier statement. 'Blues Five Spot' is a rather fast traditional blues with mild parodic overtones and a complete complement of solos. There is a peculiarity on 'Let's Cool One.' At the end of Griffin's long solo the reprise appears to loom, but at a shout from Monk the saxophonist is incited to an extended coda, into which he sardonically admits clichés from to time. Monk in his solo remains very theme-bound; this leads naturally to the reprise. 'In Walked Bud' is somewhat reminiscent of the performance with the Jazz Messengers, and again the standard order of solos is observed. 'Just a Gigolo' impresses one as a masterpiece of Monk recomposition in the form of respectful parody. 'Misterioso' here is not nearly so mysterious as the piece's first performance, or as definitive as the version with Sonny Rollins. For Griffin it is more a blowing vehicle, and as a result he succumbs to the temptation to play fast and hard. Monk's contribution remains truer to the mood of the piece. The reprise ensues naturally.

In 1984 Orrin Keepnews discovered a 'Round Midnight' that derived from the July 9 Five Spot date, and released it together with other unpublished material on *Blues Five Spot* (Milestone M-9124). Originally Monk did not want this version, with solos by him and Griffin, published, apparently since it turned out so routine. The version of 'Coming On the Hudson' represents the piece's debut. Actually, instead of Adams and Jones, Sonny Rollins and Art Blakey were to have been on hand for the recording. Monk misinformed them concerning the date. With the substitute players the band struggles through the devilish piece with its odd structure. Under other circumstances, with a thoroughly rehearsed band, Monk's arrangement of the theme should have come off bright and witty. But here the head sounds lackluster and flat. Rattled by the result, the band stops after this piece.

The version of 'Played Twice' is the first take. Despite Thad Jones' efforts on cornet the music sounds wooden and stiff. From the appearance at the Olympia in Paris on April 18, 1961 come 'Crepuscule with Nellie' and the piano solo 'Body and Soul.' There are better performances of either piece. Orrin Keepnews will have had his reasons for rescuing these recordings from the dustbin; artistic considerations were certainly not foremost among them.

Live at the Five Spot: Discovery!
Blue Note CDP 799786

Live at the Five Spot
Discovery!

John Coltrane (ts), Monk (p), Ahmed Abdul-Malik (b), Roy Haynes (d); September 11, 1958:
CREPUSCULE WITH NELLIE / TRINKLE TINKLE / IN WALKED BUD /I MEAN YOU / EPISTROPHY

Formerly it was believed that this recording was made in the summer of 1957. Recent research has indicated that it was made by Juanita (Naima) Coltrane, at a time when Johnny Griffin was actually the regular tenor in the quartet. Coltrane substituted for him when he was indisposed. The material is also included in the complete Blue Note collection, where an engineering error on the present CD which makes the tuning a half note too high is corrected. The recording was made with a portable tape machine and a single microphone. The sound is predictably substandard. Coltrane sounds much more confident than on the Jazzland recordings. For one thing, he had fully absorbed the lessons of his own Monk engagement. For another, he had evolved the personal, 'sheets of sound' style of his middle period. He in no way allows himself to be overawed by Monk. Roy Haynes' playing anticipates what later was to become the new rhythm of jazz, and so over certain stretches the performance anticipates the sound of the classic Coltrane quartet—without the latter's often tiresome modality. Monk takes evident delight in his former student's virtuosity, now brought to a new level of refinement.

The Thelonious Monk Orchestra at Town Hall
Riverside RLP 12-300; CD: OJC 135

Donald Byrd (tp), Eddie Bert (tb), Bob Northern (fr h), Jay McAllister (tu), Phil Woods (as), Charlie Rouse (ts), Pepper Adams (bs), Monk (p), Sam Jones (b), Art Taylor (d), Hall Overton (arr); February 28, 1959:
MONK'S MOOD / FRIDAY THE THIRTEENTH / LITTLE ROOTIE TOOTIE / OFF MINOR / THELONIOUS / CREPUSCULE WITH NELLIE

CD bonus tracks: THELONIOUS (unedited) / LITTLE ROOTIE
TOOTIE (encore)

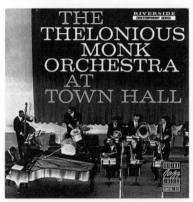

This album contains the recordings from the first concert that
Monk presented with a big band. His regular quartet is expanded
to a ten-piece outfit, for which Hall Overton wrote the arrangements, working closely with Monk. Overton respected the astrin-
gent Monk sound and orchestrates the band on the basis of his
piano style. What was only implied in the combo settings is conveyed by the orchestra here with emphatic abundance. Yet, despite my respect for the fine arrangements, I must admit to finding the earlier combo performances of the pieces more compelling in every case except 'Little Rootie Tootie.' This may be partly
owing to the fact that the ensemble of the orchestra is rather rough
and unbalanced. The recording quality, too, does little to present
the band as an organic unit. Lacking in luster, it sounds hollow, as
if emanating from a box.

The record begins with 'Thelonious.' The track is actually a
tutti version of the theme, as the edited version on record starts
with a fade-in toward the end of Monk's solo, which in the concert preceded the recapitulation. On 'Monk's Mood' the orchestra is only heard in the statement of the theme after a beautifully
phrased piano introduction, and then in the reprise. Softly the
brass leads over an airy cushion created by the reeds in the A-

sections. The saxes are silent during the B-section. Charlie Rouse is captured on disk with Monk for the first time here. His dryly elegant and rather static way of converting Monk's vertical ideas to the horizontal is already in place. Monk's own contribution works restrained variations on the theme. 'Off Minor' does not have the impact of the septet recording with Hawkins and Coltrane. The solo of Charlie Rouse is solid, with a rather conventional Monk accompaniment. The trumpet solo is not exactly a masterpiece of invention, and fails to exploit as contrasting material the occasional riffing of the A-section by the orchestra. Monk's solo is static and curt.

'Crepuscule with Nellie', solo-free as always, is also less focused than the version on *Monk's Music*, and the occasional distortion of the sax sound due to overmodulation detracts somewhat from the richly layered harmony. 'Little Rootie Tootie', despite the shortcomings of the sound-engineering, is more successful. Within the brass section the sound possibilities are exploited with a wealth of contrasts. Pepper Adams plays an outstanding solo. Donald Byrd comes off as rather static; behind his solo the orchestra riffs thematic motifs. Monk's solo is similar to that of the original performance, and Woods' is refreshingly vibrant. Thereupon the orchestra plays a very effective transcription of the piano solo on the original recording. The introduction on the record, incidentally, is taken from the encore. The sound engineer had not yet finished changing the tape spools when Monk counted off the number. So in order to have an intro to splice on later, the band played this number as an encore. This addition is on the Milestone double-album, *In Person* (M-47033), which bundles *The Thelonious Monk Orchestra at Town Hall* with *Thelonious Monk Quartet Plus Two at the Blackhawk*.

On 'Friday the 13th' the melody line is stated vigorously by the brass; the contrasting line of the original recording is played here by the reed section in juxtaposition. During the earthy solos of Rouse, Monk, Woods, and Byrd, the bass line continues to remain oriented toward the falling contrast. Only at the end of Wood's solo is there a brief interpolation from the orchestra. Art Taylor's drumming suffers from the poor recording technique, although together with Sam Jones he holds the proceedings together with admirable focus and accentuation.

Five by Monk by Five
Riverside RLP 12-305; CD: OJC 362

Thad Jones (c), Charlie Rouse (ts), Monk (p), Sam Jones (b), Art Taylor (d); June 1, 1959:
PLAYED TWICE
Same personnel; June 2, 1959:
STRAIGHT, NO CHASER / I MEAN YOU / ASK ME NOW
Same personnel; June 4, 1959:
JACKIE-ING
CD bonus tracks: PLAYED TWICE (takes 1 and 2)

Already on the drum introduction to 'Jackie-ing' it is apparent that the Riverside sound engineers of Reeves Studios had since mastered the stereo technique and were now able to produce an exceptionally realistic sound. The ensemble sounds razor sharp as it opens with a fast, four-bar bugle motif by way of introducing a theme in AA'AA' form. Monk's regular quartet was augmented for the occasion by the then Basie trumpeter, and later big band leader, Thad Jones. On this record he only plays the cornet, which has a pronounced bugle-like sound. Charlie Rouse takes the first solo. With the very tight rhythm section playing behind him, his horizontal reprocessing of Monk's strong, vertical accompaniment is engagingly to the point. Jones follows. He puts other Monk trumpeters to shame with his virtuosity and abundance of ideas grounded in tradition. In the wake of such fine interpretations of his new piece, Monk contents himself with a short, very thematic solo. In Sam Jones we have a vigorous 'walking' bassist whose lines nevertheless function as more than just substructure. As one might expect, 'Straight, No Chaser' is also performed in an earthy, bluesy style, without recourse to clichés. After Rouse and Jones, Monk is evidently pleased to play with his characteristic blues elements, while the rhythm team lends excellent support.

'Played Twice' is a medium-fast, typically Monkish melody that appears rhythmically plain, but is actually complex. It is in AABA form, and is run through twice. It seems simple because each section is only four bars each. Thad Jones has the first solo. Although the tempo does not particularly appeal to him, he acquits himself ably. For Rouse and of course Monk the tempo is ideal. Before the solid bass background Monk is again very spare. The Milestone double album *Brilliance* (M-47023) contains, besides the recordings of *Brilliant Corners* (less 'I Surrender Dear') and *Five by Monk by Five*, yet another take of 'Played Twice.'

'I Mean You' is a Monk classic and is handled informally. Thad Jones has the first solo. The piano accompaniment prods him into the desired Monk corners. Charlie Rouse needs no prompting from the piano during his own solo. When Jones checks back in, Monk refrains from commenting, and the same during Rouse's second statement. The piano solo begins spare and abstract, then, in a manner reminiscent of Basie, Monk recapitulates the melody with a succession of chords before the reprise.

'Ask Me Now' is another classic Monk composition. It is presented in fast ballad tempo. The trumpet and saxophone declaim the theme in unison. Monk's solo creates a quiet space before the double time of the drums. Although it is gratifying that *Five by Monk by Five* does not adhere to the strict order of solos followed by the regular quartet, it is nevertheless too bad that Sam Jones, in especially good form here, is not given an opportunity to solo.

Thelonious Alone in San Francisco
Riverside RLP 12-312; CD: OJC 231

Monk (p solo); October 21, 1959:
PANNONICA / BLUE MONK / EVERYTHING HAPPENS TO
ME / ROUND LIGHTS / RUBY, MY DEAR / THERE'S DAN-
GER IN YOUR EYES, CHERIE (take 2)
Same, October 22, 1959:
REMEMBER / REFLECTIONS / BLUEHAWK / YOU TOOK
THE WORDS RIGHT OUT OF MY HEART
CD bonus tracks: THERE'S DANGER IN YOUR EYES,
CHERIE (take 1)

This is the second solo album that Monk recorded for Riverside. In mood and temperament it is not unlike *Thelonious Himself.* Here, too, the standards are presented rubato without any haste or hurry. Yet in their execution the beat is always clearly marked, and in that respect the recordings are a sequel to the Paris solo album, but without the harsh, almost brittle determination of the latter. Not even the Monk tunes played with an explicit beat have that Parisian quality; on the contrary, there is a playfulness about them, as when the left hand on 'Blue Monk' suddenly sketches a stride figure. The first performance of 'Round Lights' is a refined, free playing with blues elements, without a distinctive melody. 'Bluehawk' on the other hand is a genuine blues, based on a riff motif; after 'Blue Monk' it is the piece with the most pronounced beat. It helps with the variety on the album that beside the prevalent ballad tempos a few faster tempi turn up. On this account alone this solo album is more exciting than *Thelonious Himself.*

Thelonious Monk Quartet Plus Two at the Blackhawk
Riverside RLP 12-323; CD: OJC 305

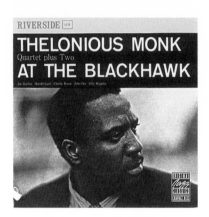

Joe Gordon (tp), Harold Land and Charlie Rouse (ts), Monk (p), John Ore (b), Billy Higgins (d); April 29, 1960:
LET'S CALL THIS / FOUR IN ONE / I'M GETTING SENTI-MENTAL OVER YOU / WORRY LATER (SAN FRANCISCO HOLIDAY) / 'ROUND MIDNIGHT / EPISTROPHY (theme)
CD bonus tracks: EPISTROPHY (in full) / EVIDENCE

Evidence
Milestone M-9115
Selections and personnel listed below

The Riverside album was actually supposed to document a meeting in San Francisco between Monk and the popular West Coast drummer Shelly Manne. Joe Gordon played with Manne, and Harold Land, who had worked with Clifford Brown and Max Roach, was brought up from Los Angeles. In the event, the collaboration of Monk and Manne set off no sparks, and so it was decided to record the regular quartet, to which drummer Billy Higgins belonged at the time, with Manne and both guest horn players, on an evening during Monk's guest spot at the Blackhawk in San Francisco. Listening to Billy Higgins, this master of tasteful, light-footed swing in the Kenny Clarke tradition, one wonders why anyone would want to replace him—even for a collaboration with such publicity value. One infers from the recording that the guest players were taught Monk's themes by Charlie Rouse in a hurry. They acquit themselves ably enough but without much imagination in their solos. The possibilities of the sextet setting remain unexploited in the theme arrangements, and so the album has the character of a blowing session based on Monk tunes. Of some interest is the first performance of 'Worry Later', which on later recordings appears as 'San Francisco Holiday.' The Latin-inspired AABA theme is declaimed by the horns in eighth-notes. It is then treated rather straightforwardly. As the first soloist Rouse strolls on in his typically solid, unspectacular fashion. Joe Gordon plays competently, yet without exciting the audience, his lines being rather conventional. Harold Land plays fluidly, more in the style of Parker than Rouse, and without the latter's deep understanding of Monk. Monk, in his turn, performs rather conventionally as well. On ''Round Midnight' Monk and the horns are more inspired.

Perhaps the record would be more than the document of an interesting club date if Billy Higgins had as fine a partner in John Ore as Art Taylor before him had in Sam Jones. Yet Ore seems to have finally represented Monk's ideal: a bassist who could be relied upon to provide the harmonic framework of a piece, but from whom no great imaginative impulse was to be expected. He does not venture on any solos during this evening at the Blackhawk.

This was the last Monk album to be produced by Orrin Keepnews at Riverside. It is not at the conceptual level of Monk's other Riverside productions. It is included in the Milestone double album *In Person* (M-47033), together with *The Thelonious Monk Orchestra at Town Hall.*

On *Evidence*, material from the Blackhawk engagement and the Town Hall concert is included. 'In Walked Bud', 'Blue Monk', and 'Rhythm-a-ning' are the numbers that the quartet at the Town Hall concert played for the sound check. The performances are predictably loose. 'Thelonious' is performed with the complete big band at full length. From The Blackhawk there is an alternate take of 'San Francisco Holiday' (aka 'Worry Later'), 'Evidence' and 'Epistrophy.'

Monk in France
Riverside 9491; CD: OJC 670

Charlie Rouse (ts), Monk (p), John Ore (b), Frankie Dunlop (d); Paris, April 18, 1961:
EPISTROPHY / APRIL IN PARIS (p solo) / I'M GETTING SENTIMENTAL OVER YOU / JUST A GIGOLO (p solo) / I MEAN YOU (edited on LP) / JACKIE-ING / OFF MINOR / RHYTHM-A-NING / HACKENSACK / WELL, YOU NEEDN'T
CD bonus tracks: BODY AND SOUL (p solo) / CREPUSCULE WITH NELLIE

Monk in Italy
Riverside 9443; CD OJC 488

Same personnel; Milan, April 21, 1961:
JACKIE-ING / EPISTROPHY / BODY AND SOUL (p solo) / STRAIGHT, NO CHASER / BEMSHA SWING / SAN FRANCISCO HOLIDAY / CREPUSCULE WITH NELLIE
CD bonus track: RHYTHM-A-NING

Two Hours with Thelonious
Riverside 9460/1
Complete contents of two previous LPs.

The Monk quartet in this particular lineup had been in existence nearly a year when they embarked on their first European tour. In Paris they appeared in the legendary music hall Olympia and were broadcast on French radio (which explains the mono recording). Monk seems to be in good spirits revisiting the site of his first European trip. The quartet received enthusiastic notices on this occasion, and many critics hailed them as representatives of the avant-garde.

In retrospect this view cannot be maintained, not only by comparison with contemporary developments in jazz originating with Cecil Taylor and Ornette Coleman, but also from the perspective of Monk's own work to date. The quartet's repertoire consisted mainly of classics from the pianist's early creative period. And since he now worked almost exclusively with this quartet, his well broken-in unit, he no longer had challenging encounters with new and distinctive musical personalities such as Sonny Rollins, Coleman Hawkins, John Coltrane, Johnny Griffin, and Gerry Mulligan. It is certainly wrong in Charlie Rouse's case, for instance, to gainsay his individuality. But his individuality consisted precisely in his fidelity to the material, and his ability to give horizontal expression to Monk's vertically and elliptically conceived ideas.

For the discriminating listener, to be sure, the symbiosis between pianist and horn player, which served to faithfully mediate the composer's intention, remained interesting for years to come. But the performance of the same material with the same personnel and the same musical approach naturally runs the risk of becoming tedious. Some critics feel that Monk's new rhythm team was partly responsible for this. They have invidiously compared the more conceptually daring rhythm sections that Miles Davis and John Coltrane had at the time. Some have dismissed the close-knit statement of the pulse by bass and drums in the Monk quartet as almost comic in the way it bounced along squarely on the beat. But this is to ignore the mesmerizing liveliness of the quartet's rhythmic concept. It is this rhythmic concept that largely accounts for the freshness the music still has today.

In Paris in 1961 the new rhythm team inspired the whole band with good humor, and Monk's solos are exuberant. His brief, unaccompanied performances of 'Just a Gigolo' and especially 'April in Paris' are in the same spirit. His enthusiasm affects the audience and fellow musicians, catches fire, and carries through 'I Mean You', 'Jackie-ing', 'Off Minor', Rhythm-a-ning', 'Hackensack', and 'Well, You Needn't.' None of these are boring, despite being presented in the hackneyed formula 'theme, tenor solo, piano solo, (walking) bass solo, drum solo, theme.' The high level of inspiration even carries over to the bass and drums, despite their operating as mere slaves to the rhythm.

The Paris concert is also obtainable on the Milestone double album *April in Paris / Live* (M-47060). The sound quality of the Milan concert is inferior, more hollow, though the recording is in stereo. In his unaccompanied performance of 'Body and Soul' Monk explores the structure of the original more profoundly than he did on his playful solo performance of the piece in Paris. In general these Milan performances helped solidify a reputation for performance at the highest level at a time when the quartet was receiving great public acclaim.

All Riverside, Milestone, and Jazzland recordings, together with many alternate and breakdown takes, are on:

Thelonious Monk: The Complete Riverside Recordings
Riverside 022 (15 CDs)

Here, in addition to all the performances mentioned there is also a 'Bye-Ya' with the 'Epistrophy' theme appended. It was recorded July 9, 1958 at the Five Spot. On it, Art Blakey substituted for Roy Haynes in a guest appearance at the end of the evening. He is very familiar with the composition, although in the presentation of the theme he seems uncertain whether the arrangement he knew was still in effect. Overall it is reminiscent of the spirit of the Blue Note and (especially) Atlantic recordings that they made together. Blakey with his earthy style certainly proves himself the more congenial Monk drummer than the more refined Roy Haynes. It is a shame that the recording engineer fails to capture the full force of Blakey's sound. From an August 7, 1958 recording date at the Five Spot there is also a previously unreleased version of 'Evidence'.

Live in Stockholm 1961
Dragon 151/152; CD: DIW 315/6

Charlie Rouse (ts), Monk (p), John Ore (b), Frankie Dunlop (d); May 16, 1961:
JACKIE-ING / I'M GETTING SENTIMENTAL OVER YOU / CREPUSCULE WITH NELLIE / BA-LUE BOLIVAR BA-LUES-ARE / RHYTHM-A-NING / EPISTROPHY / JUST A GIGOLO / WELL, YOU NEEDN'T / 'ROUND MIDNIGHT / BLUE MONK / EPISTROPHY / BODY AND SOUL

The band on this date is clearly inspired by the enthusiastic response their tour of Europe had been receiving up to then. Moreover, they had performed together long enough to be capable of playing off each other in their sleep (but not so long as to be bored of doing so). It is fortunate that the sequence of songs in the concert is preserved on the record. The excellent sound quality illuminates a performance that surpasses the Paris and Milan dates. 'Just a Gigolo' and 'Body and Soul' are performed solo, as usual.

Live at the Village Gate
Xanadu LP 202; CD 5161

Charlie Rouse (ts), Monk (p), John Ore (b), Frankie Dunlop (d); late summer 1962 (the date given, December 11, 1963 is highly unlikely):
RHYTHM-A-NING / BODY AND SOUL / I'M GETTING SENTIMENTAL OVER YOU / BODY AND SOUL / JACKIE-ING

This is a somewhat obscure live recording of mediocre sound quality. The mood in the club is enthusiastic, even passionate, and the band responds in kind. Even Thelonious cannot resist throwing in some flashy, crowd-pleasing phrases. Unfortunately his piano is not well-tuned, but this seems to provoke him to greater heights of defiant imaginativeness. Both versions of 'Body and Soul' are performed solo, the second time much more slowly.

The Columbia Years

The CBS recordings are listed with the original stereo numbers, most beginning 'Columbia CS...' Nearly all are available on CD, but unfortunately mostly without bonus tracks. The CDs have the same covers as the original LPs, but different catalog numbers. From the beginning, Teo Macero's practice with CBS was not to produce albums carefully conceived beforehand, but to take Monk into the studio at regular intervals and collect the material on disc at a later date.

This section of the discography includes some live recordings made during the years Monk was under contract with Columbia, but subsequently issued by different labels.

Monk's Dream
Columbia CS 8765; CD: Columbia 40786

*Charlie Rouse (ts), Monk (p), John Ore (b), Frankie Dunlop (d);
October 31, 1962:*
BYE-YA
Same personnel; November 1, 1962:
BOLIVAR BLUES / BRIGHT MISSISSIPPI / BODY AND SOUL (p solo)
Same personnel; November 2, 1962:
MONK'S DREAM / JUST A GIGOLO (p solo)
Same personnel; November 6, 1962:
SWEET AND LOVELY / FIVE SPOT BLUES

Monk's Dream is Thelonious Monk's debut on CBS. The concept is the same as that of *Two Hours with Thelonious.* The quartet is recorded with perfect studio fidelity. Frankie Dunlop's drum playing now meshes superbly with the solos. He also does a good job of highlighting the odd accents in the themes. Together with John Ore they fashion a lightly jumping, right-on-the-beat rhythmic style that became a distinctive characteristic of the Monk quartet.

The title piece is first on the album. It is a simply constructed AABA song theme, introduced by the piano in medium-fast tempo in a trio setting. Charlie Rouse only appears as a soloist. He, like the others, seems particularly inspired. Monk's own solo toys with the theme, which is then presented *tutti* in the reprise. 'Body and Soul' is a piano solo. In slow bounce-tempo the right hand plays variations on the theme, while the left jumps in traditional stride style.

'Bright Mississippi' is obviously and ironically based on the Dixieland chestnut 'Sweet Georgia Brown.' Charlie Rouse has the first solo. Monk goads him with his typical spare chord clusters. His own solo is full of fun, in the way it mostly avoids quoting the theme and occasionally throws in his two-hand devices. He finally does paraphrase the theme, to prepare for the reprise. On 'Five Spot Blues' Rouse is more adventuresome. Monk is intense in the way he rearranges elements of the theme, and Dunlop fills every gap like a finely tuned watch. Monk surprises with a boogie-style introduction to 'Bolivar Blues' (formerly 'Ba-lue Bolivar Ba-lues-are'). The saxophone solo again develops against the backdrop of a dense piano accompaniment. Monk begins his solo with almost hackneyed eighth-note triplets, but then boldly develops those implications with quarter-note triplets, posed as a challenge against the undeviating march of the rhythm section. This version, by virtue of his solo, clearly surpasses the original on *Brilliant Corners*, as good as that is. 'Just a Gigolo' is also a tad more venturesome here than in earlier renditions.

'Bye-Ya' is taken at a torrid pace. Rouse plays in close alliance with Monk. Monk's solo is at first prosaically thematic, until his irrepressible humor blazes forth, leading to the reprise. 'Sweet and Lovely' is introduced with slight variations by the piano in a trio setting. The tempo deliberately drags. Monk plays a long solo, during which the left hand repeatedly jumps. His accompaniment behind the saxophone solo is so dense that one could legitimately speak of a duet. The reprise is again handled by Monk in trio; Charlie Rouse occasionally fortifies the bass of the piano with unison notes.

Monk's Dream is aptly named: it represents his leadership of an ensemble imbued to the highest degree with his musical personality. The ensemble playing of this quartet was remarkable, and their every interaction, down to the least accent in the drums, was informed by Monk's world of sound. It is as if they were just waiting for this recording date to proclaim their identity. The music is distilled to its essence. There are no superfluous 'filler' solos.

Criss Cross
Columbia CS 8838; CD: Columbia 469184

Charlie Rouse (ts), Monk (p), John Ore (b), Frankie Dunlop (d); November 6, 1962:

HACKENSACK / RHYTHM-A-NING
Same personnel; February 26, 1963:
TEA FOR TWO (without Rouse) / CRISS CROSS
Same personnel; February 27, 1963:
ERONEL / DON'T BLAME ME (p solo)
Same personnel; February 28, 1963:
THINK OF ONE
Same personnel; March 29, 1963:
CREPUSCULE WITH NELLIE
CD bonus track: PANNONICA

Criss Cross is a pendant to *Monk's Dream.* On two pieces the re-cording dates overlap. In general Monk's CBS albums were not the products of an antecedent concept, realized in the studio in more or less a single session. CBS was more in the habit of bring-ing Monk into the studio on a regular basis, then releasing albums composed of accumulated material. Material that got overlooked at the time was later released on *Always Know*, containing music from 1962 to 1968.

The mood of the music and the playfulness of the band on *Criss Cross* and *Monk's Dream* largely correspond. *Criss Cross* does not contain any new compositions. But Monk understandably wanted to use his earlier compositions to create a new interna-tional audience, an opportunity made possible by the exposure CBS provided him. Many of his older recordings were out of print, and now he had an ensemble devoted to his sound concep-tion, which could execute his ideas blindfolded. His master com-position 'Criss Cross' has a B-section reduced to the first six bars, and this economy makes the performance as a whole more com-pelling than the debut recording. The other pieces also forego full solos on the part of the bass and drums of the kind often indulged in live. It is interesting to compare 'Tea for Two' with the trio version on *The Unique.* The new performance is somewhat more engaging with its accelerated tempo, and John Ore has a great moment in his plucked bass intro. Frankie Dunlop finally translates to the drums every rhythmic implication of the piano. His almost daily association with Monk, extended over years, had made the pianist's rhythmic conception second nature to him. 'Don't Blame Me' is a very beautiful, extended piano solo in leisurely tempo, with a moderate amount of stride accompaniment in the left hand, while the right plays conventional trill figures.

Tokyo Concerts
Columbia 38510; CD: 466552

Charlie Rouse (ts), Monk (p), Butch Warren (b), Frankie Dunlop (d); May 21, 1963:
STRAIGHT, NO CHASER / PANNONICA / JUST A GIGOLO (p solo) / EVIDENCE /JACKIE-ING / BEMSHA SWING / EPISTROPHY (theme) / I'M GETTING SENTIMENTAL OVER YOU / HACKENSACK / BLUE MONK / EPISTROPHY

In May 1963 the quartet toured Japan, to great acclaim. Instead of John Ore, the bassist was Butch Warren. His rhythmic approach resembles that of his predecessor—which is to say, that of Monk—but his tone is livelier and has greater drive. The quartet gave two spirited concerts on May 21 in Tokyo's Sankei Hall. The results are captured on a double album. Urged on by the crowd the band embarks on an earthy 'Straight, No Chaser.' The execution reflects Monk's live ritual. Frankie Dunlop's solo, following the solidly 'walked' bass solo, is much more than routine, and tastefully melodic. In the provocative live atmosphere his accompaniments, on the other hand, often come off pushy and obtrusive. On 'Evidence' Charlie Rouse sheds his usual reserve. Piano and drums methodically propel him to new heights, where he remains even without the piano accompaniment. Monk's solo has the character of a melodic and rhythmic ping-pong game with the percussion *con* bass accompaniment.

   After the snappy drum intro and the statement of the theme, sparks fly on the quick tempoed 'Jackie-ing.' Warren and Dunlop are so busy that Monk leaves it to them to accompany Rouse. Monk's solo again gives the impression of a duet with the drums. Here again, as on 'Evidence', the music gains in unity by forego-ing another walking bass solo. 'Bemsha Swing', with its daring piano accompaniment–out of phase, as it were–and the crisp drum accents during the head, is more satisfying than most earlier per-formances of the piece. On 'I'm Getting Sentimental Over You' and 'Hackensack' the quartet is less driven by the piano, but sounds more relaxed. 'Hackensack' contains another walking bass solo, followed by drum solo, and again the drums sound more me-lodic. On 'Blue Monk' the mood is relaxed, humorous and bluesy. All members of the quartet solo. Warren works an interesting varia-tion on the walking motif. Monk and Rouse are the only soloists on a complete version of 'Epistrophy.' Monk develops his motifs in a complex, extended solo, that brings the double album to an impressive close.

Monk Misterioso
CBS CS 9216; CD: Columbia 468406

Charlie Rouse (ts), Monk (p), Butch Warren (b), Frankie Dunlop (d); Tokyo, May 21, 1963:
EVIDENCE
Same personnel; Newport, July 4, 1963:
LIGHT BLUE
Charlie Rouse (ts), Monk (p), Larry Gales (b), Ben Riley (d); Los Angeles, November 1, 1964:
I'M GETTING SENTIMENTAL OVER YOU / ALL THE THINGS YOU ARE
Same personnel; San Francisco, November 4, 1964:
BEMSHA SWING
Same personnel; Brandeis University, February 27, 1965:
WELL, YOU NEEDN'T
Same personnel but without Rouse; CBS Studio, March 2, 1965:
HONEYSUCKLE ROSE

One might suppose that *Misterioso* is a meal of leftovers. In fact it is a collection of first-class live material, none of which had been released up to that point. It covers the period May 1963 to March 1965. Apparently the idea for the album arose from the circumstance that Monk was only in the studio on two brief occasions in 1965, and CBS did not have enough material for a studio album. The fact that the information on the sleeve omits four titles, and that the studio recording of 'Honeysuckle Rose' is furnished with artificial applause to make it sound like a live recording, attest to CBS' diminished interest in Monk during the second half of the sixties.

'Well, You Needn't' shows that, despite having new personnel on bass and drums, the rhythmic approach of the quartet remained unchanged. The solos vary in quality and none is especially inspired. 'Misterioso' derives from the triumphant *Big Band and Quartet* concert in Lincoln Hall in 1963. Although the complex interplay between piano and soloists that marked the debut recording is missing, replaced by a far more conventional accompaniment, the performance succeeds by virtue of the relaxed interpretation of Charlie Rouse, who plays without piano accompaniment after the first choruses. Monk's solo does bring to mind some of the elements of the first performance. 'Light Blue' was performed at the Newport Festival with the same personnel. In his accompaniment to Monk's solo John Ore for once doesn't rely on his usual walk patterns.

'I'm Getting Sentimental Over You' is a decent club performance, but one can hear it done better on other CBS records. The handling of the old popular song 'All the Things You Are' is interesting precisely because it is so conventional. Monk largely foregoes accompaniment behind Rouse, and in his own solo paraphrases the theme with his typical seconds. 'Honeysuckle Rose' is performed in a trio, and perfectly recorded. It is treated as a joke, yet comes off as more than parody. The performance of the same tune on *The Unique* is superior, however. The simplified presentation of the theme in the interpretation of 'Bemsha Swing' offered here immediately suggests that it is less definitive than the performance at the Tokyo concert of 1963. With a version of 'Evidence' from this latter concert this uneven album concludes. *Misterioso* at least makes one thing clear: the 1963 version of the quartet with Warren and Dunlop represented a high point in the history of Rouse and Monk's collaboration.

Miles Davis/Thelonious Monk Live at Newport
CD: Columbia C2 K 53585

Charlie Rouse (ts), Pee Wee Russell (cl), Monk (p), Butch Warren (b), Frankie Dunlop (d); July 4, 1963:
NUTTY / BLUE MONK
Charlie Rouse (ts), Monk (p), Butch Warren (b), Frankie Dunlop (d); July 4, 1963:
CRISS CROSS /LIGHT BLUE / EPISTROPHY

The title is misleading since Miles and Monk are represented by selections from their appearances at Newport in different years, and they don't perform together. Only the titles on which Monk plays are listed above. The two numbers on which Chicago-style clarinetist Pee Wee Russell plays have the value of a curiosity.

Russell had a genuine interest in modern jazz. He is clearly lost on 'Nutty', yet somehow keeps from falling flat on his face. Monk's rhythm section supports him before and behind. The playing of the Monk team is not very imaginative, though certainly long-winded. On 'Blue Monk' Russell is more at home with the blues, but Monk's band is stuck in routine.

The double CD version of the concert adds the three tracks by the Monk quartet. The other CD documents a performance at the 1958 Newport Festival by the classic Miles Davis sextet with John Coltrane, Cannonball Adderly, Wynton Kelly, Paul Chambers, and Jimmy Cobb.

Live at the Monterey Jazz Festival, 1963
Jazz Unlimited CD 2045/46; Storyville 2CD 8255/56

Charlie Rouse (ts), Monk (p), John Ore (b), Frankie Dunlop (d); September 21, 1963:
I'M GETTING SENTIMENTAL OVER YOU / WELL, YOU NEEDN'T / LIGHT BLUE / CRISS CROSS / EPISTROPHY
Charlie Rouse (ts), Monk (p), John Ore (b), Frankie Dunlop (d); September 22, 1963:
EVIDENCE / I MEAN YOU / SWEET AND LOVELY / BRIGHT MISSISSIPPI

The doubts concerning this recording, which does not appear in most discographies, have been dispelled by the specialist Fred Canté, who confirmed its authenticity. So we can safely enjoy a musically as well as technically superior performance. The players are in fine form. The interplay of Ore and Dunlop is especially good and is documented for the last time here on record. Dunlop's beats and accents are as nonchalant as can be, yet explode sharply and squarely on the beat.

Monk Big Band and Quartet in Concert
CD Columbia 476898

Charlie Rouse (ts), Thad Jones (c), Nick Travis (tp), Eddie Bert (tb),
Steve Lacy (ss), Phil Woods (as, cl), Gene Allen (bs, cl, b cl), Monk (p),
Butch Warren (b), Frankie Dunlop (d), Hall Overton (arr); December
30, 1963:
I MEAN YOU / EVIDENCE / DARKNESS ON THE DELTA (p
solo) / PLAYED TWICE (quartet) / OSKA T. / FOUR IN ONE /
EPISTROPHY (theme) / BYE-YA / MISTERIOSO / EPISTRO-
PHY (theme) / LIGHT BLUE

This double CD reproduces the concert in its entirety. The bass
solos and several exciting drum solos are unabridged. The supe-
riority of this big band over the one at the Town Hall concert is
immediately apparent on the first piece, 'I Mean You.' The kernel
of the band, Monk's regular quartet, is incomparably better co-
ordinated than his 1959 quartet, and the whole outfit is better
rehearsed. (CBS' budget may be responsible.) Thad Jones is the
superior trumpeter (or cornettist, in this case), and the replace-
ment of a French horn by a second trumpet gives the mix more
bite. Last but not least, the quality of the recording is improved.

Under these conditions Hall Overton's fine arrangements
could be realized in all their beauty. Even when the big band
plays select chords behind the solos, the sound remains unobtru-
sive and never becomes bombastic. The rhythm section is also
thoroughly Monkish in its approach. One might regret the some-

what rigid assignment of solos to Thad Jones, Charlie Rouse, Monk, Phil Woods, and then John Ore and Frankie Dunlop, in view of the presence of Steve Lacy in the saxophone section. Yet the soloists play with imagination and verve. A great addition is the new Monk composition 'Oska T' (a garbled rendering of 'Ask for tea', or 'T' for Thelonious). It consists of a two-bar riff repeated three times, followed by a two-bar tag. This whole eight-bar complex is repeated four times. The possibility inherent in the form as a faintly oriental, modally tinged, vamp-style 'springboard' is ably exploited without resorting to clichés, especially with and behind the cornet solo. 'Four in One' sounds magnificent in this big band setting. After Monk's solo there is a complex *tutti* passage based on a Monk solo, which the ensemble plays with astonishing precision. 'Epistrophy' is served up in condensed form without solos, as a sophisticated way of announcing intermission.

All the pieces of this big band recording are of a welcome freshness, and display a thoroughly Monkish love of variety. (In the quartet context these moments became less frequent.) The remaining performances, including a very relaxed yet focused 'Misterioso', are on the same high level of execution, making this one of Monk's best albums overall.

It's Monk's Time
Columbia CS 8984; CD: Columbia 468405

Monk (p); January 29, 1964:
NICE WORK IF YOU CAN GET IT
Charlie Rouse (ts), Monk (p), Butch Warren (b), Ben Riley (d); January 30, 1964:
STUFFY TURKEY
Same personnel; February 10, 1964:
LULU'S BACK IN TOWN / BRAKE'S SAKE
Same personnel; March 9, 1964:
MEMORIES OF YOU (p solo) / SHUFFLE BOIL

It's Monk's Time was Monk's first album with the drummer Ben Riley. Compared with his predecessor, Frankie Dunlop, he makes greater use of the cymbal, with a more supple and flexible swing. In his solos it is plain that Roy Haynes, with his graceful elegance, was his great exemplar. The trend away from hardness or pungency, and toward grace and playful elegance, characterizes the whole album. 'Lulu's Back in Town' is the first piece. It opens with an extended, unaccompanied piano solo, in which the theme is stated and then varied in jump-style, in almost caricaturizing manner. The theme is then repeated *tutti*, and Charlie Rouse plays a long, theme-oriented solo, during the second half of which the piano sits out. Ben Riley claims the second solo; he invokes the thematic structure of the piece with a refined feeling for the drums' dynamics. Monk plays the reprise unaccompanied. An elegantly reserved sound was already evident in the playing of the piano intro, and one is not surprised to hear the same sound engineered into the *tutti* passages. A trace of echo in the saxophone and drums, pushed somewhat into the background with respect to the cymbals, together with a rounded bass sound, gives the playing of the quartet a distinction unknown to it before. Monk himself seems to have consciously contributed to the genteel mood. His solo interpretations of 'Memories of You' and 'Nice Work If You Can Get It' impress one as respectful and only mildly exotic stride exercises.

'On Stuffy Turkey', an almost disappointingly simple AABA song, the relaxed atmosphere is such that during the saxophone's statement of the theme a measure is simply omitted from the B-section. In his solo Rouse plays around the A-section riff. The piano solo is limited to a sequence of chords not much more original. The drum contributes an enjoyably hip solo, before the theme reprise—this time less the saxophone in the B-section—closes the first side.

'Brake's Sake' is an exceptionally original melody in Monk's best manner. The sections consist of contrasting four-bar motifs, arranged in AABB order. The tenor solo comes first, in close association with the piano, which leaves off once it has firmly imposed the composer's ideal of sound. Monk's solo is intense and hard-working, leaving no doubt that he is leader of the band. Unfortunately this intensity is not matched by the bass, but Monk just works that much harder. Perhaps Butch Warren was preoccupied planning his own solo, which he then plays with surprising agility. Ben Riley next demonstrates anew his talent for the subtle, melodic drum solo.

After 'Nice Work If You Can Get It' comes 'Shuffle Boil.' Monk had recorded this once before, in 1955, as a sideman with Gigi Gryce. (The same is true of 'Brake's Sake'). In the treble section it is another simple AABA song, but the contrasting bass sections in the piano, which leads to unorthodox accenting of the melody in the A-section, makes this a typically angular Monk theme. On the debut performance (*Gigi Gryce Quartet*) this angularity is beautifully exploited, owing to the parallel articulation of contrasting phrases in the contrabass and piano. In the quartet performance these contrary movements are not so highlighted, but they are a subject of the saxophone solo. The recording technique helps to distinguish the individual voices. Thus the interplay between Rouse and Monk, Monk and Riley, and Warren and Riley, together with Riley's solo, emerge with particular clarity.

Live in Paris, Alhambra, 1964 Volume 1
France's Concert FC 135; CD FCD 135

Charlie Rouse (ts), Monk (p), Butch Warren (b), Ben Riley (d); February 22, 1964:
STUFFY TURKEY / BRAKE'S SAKE / BLUE MONK / RUBY, MY DEAR / RHYTHM-A-NING / EPISTROPHY (theme)

Live in Paris, 1964
France's Concert FCD 132/2

Charlie Rouse (ts), Monk (p), Butch Warren (b), Ben Riley (d);
February 23, 1964:
FOUR IN ONE / I'M GETTING SENTIMENTAL OVER YOU /
STRAIGHT, NO CHASER / [UNIDENTIFIED DRUM SOLO
(not on the directory of titles)] / WELL, YOU NEEDN'T /
EPISTROPHY / BLUE MONK / SWEET AND LOVELY /
HACKENSACK / RHYTHM-A-NING / BRIGHT MISSISSIPPI
/ EPISTROPHY (theme)

The first concert took place in the famous revue-theater, the
Alhambra. The piano is woefully out of tune. Monk battles it with
a will, and even appears energized by the liability. In the second,
which took place in the house of the O.R.T.F., the French state
radio, the piano is in better condition, and the music is duller.

Monk
Columbia CS 9091; CD: Columbia 468407

Charlie Rouse (ts), Monk (p), Butch Warren (b), Ben Riley (d); March
9, 1964:
TEO
Charlie Rouse (ts), Monk (p), Larry Gales (b), Ben Riley (d); October
6, 1964:
LIZA / (JUST ONE WAY TO SAY) I LOVE YOU (p solo)
Same personnel; October 7, 1964:
THAT OLD MAN (CHILDREN'S SONG)
Same personnel; October 8, 1964:
PANNONICA / JUST YOU JUST ME / APRIL IN PARIS

Like *It's Monk's Time,* this album is also distinguished by relative
conservatism and elegance. In the quartet numbers (except for
'Teo') Larry Gales replaces Butch Warren on bass. It is soon evident that he went beyond Monk's ideal of a pure timekeeper in

the 'walking' mode. With the appearance of *Monk, Down Beat* appropriately wrote: 'As Monk rattles over familiar territory, we recognize an old friend serious in his humor, predictable in his unpredictability, comfortable in his discomfort.' One has only to add that the entire Monk team is found playing with their usual sense of fun, so that 'April in Paris', this time offered in a quartet setting, and the children's song 'That Old Man', give particular satisfaction.

'I Love You' is a playful stride outing you might imagine hearing at a rowdy party. *Down Beat*'s overall judgment applies particularly to 'Just You Just Me': 'Rouse plays with consistency and competence, but little more.' Most listeners enjoyed the masterful Monk composition 'Pannonica' for the first time with this album, although the superior debut recording (on *Brilliant Corners*) was still available. 'Teo' is a pithy ABA composition that derives from the same recording date that produced the arresting 'Shuffle Boil' on *It's Monk's Time*. The density and economy of 'Teo' make it the best thing on *Monk*, with theme, tenor solo, piano solo, theme—and not a wasted phrase.

Solo Monk
Columbia CS 9149; CD: Columbia 471248

Monk (p); October 31, 1964:
I SURRENDER DEAR / SWEET AND LOVELY / EVERY-
THING HAPPENS TO ME / I SHOULD CARE / NORTH OF
THE SUNSET
Same; November 2, 1964:
THESE FOOLISH THINGS / I HADN'T ANYONE TILL YOU
/ DINAH / I'M CONFESSIN' THAT I LOVE YOU / MONK'S
POINT
Same; February 23, 1965:
ASK ME NOW
Same; March 2, 1965:
RUBY, MY DEAR
CD bonus track: INTROSPECTION

Solo numbers are a feature of all Monk's CBS productions, but at
the end of October 1964 the company decided to produce a pure
piano album with him. The basic idea was to showcase Monk's
place in the stride tradition. The song selection concentrates on
standards. Notable is the statement of the theme on 'Monk's Point',
a traditional blues riff theme. With his peculiar way of striking the
keys, Monk achieves an especially arresting note-bending effect.
Unfortunately Monk was not in good form on the October and
November recording dates; he delivers the pieces indifferently,
as if it were a duty and an imposition. The judgment of *Down Beat*
is on the money: 'CBS should not have released these recordings..., especially since Monk has played most of these pieces much
better in the past.'

Thelonious Monk Live at the It Club
Columbia C2 38030; CD: Columbia 469186-2

*Charlie Rouse (ts), Monk (p), Larry Gales (b), Ben Riley (d); October
31, 1964:*
BLUE MONK / WELL, YOU NEEDN'T / 'ROUND MID-
NIGHT / RHYTHM-A-NING / BLUES FIVE SPOT / BEMSHA
SWING / STRAIGHT, NO CHASER / EVIDENCE / NUTTY

Same personnel; November 1, 1964:
MISTERIOSO / GALLOP'S GALLOP / BA-LUE BOLIVAR BA-
LUES-ARE

Thelonious Monk Live at the Jazz Workshop
Columbia C2 38269; CD: Columbia 469183-2

*Charlie Rouse (ts), Monk (p), Larry Gales (b), Ben Riley (d); Novem-
ber 3, 1964:*
DON'T BLAME ME (p solo) / BA-LUE BOLIVAR BA-LUES-ARE
/ WELL, YOU NEEDN'T / EVIDENCE / RHYTHM-A-NING
(medley) / 'ROUND MIDNIGHT / I'M GETTING SENTIMEN-
TAL OVER YOU / MEMORIES OF YOU (p solo) / JUST YOU
JUST ME
Same personnel; November 4, 1964:
BLUE MONK / BRIGHT MISSISSIPPI / EPISTROPHY /
BEMSHA SWING / HACKENSACK / MISTERIOSO

After Monk's death, CBS decided to release a double album of
tracks from his west coast appearances in late 1964 at the It Club
in Los Angeles and the Jazz Workshop in San Francisco. Only
three pieces had been originally judged worthy of release, on
Misterioso. In the friendly and stimulating club atmosphere Monk
is clearly in better spirits than on the contemporary studio dates
for his solo albums. Nevertheless, his playing of these same classic originals is better on earlier albums. Rouse and the rhythm
section still play deftly and powerfully, without resorting to the
sorts of clichés that often impress an audience. Of especial interest is 'Gallop's Gallop', which to that point had only been available in the version on *Nica's Tempo* with the Gigi Gryce quartet. It
is a difficult, bebop-influenced AABA composition in medium-
fast tempo with a strong B-section related to the A-section. Both
these albums offer representative glimpses into Monk's live appearances at the time. The sound quality lags behind studio standards, especially on the recordings from the It Club.

The Great Canadian Concert of the Thelonious Monk Quartet
Can-Am 1100

Charlie Rouse (ts), Monk (p), Larry Gales (b), Ben Riley (d); August 21, 1965:
LIGHT BLUE / STRAIGHT, NO CHASER / HACKENSACK / BLUE MONK / APRIL IN PARIS / EVIDENCE / EPISTRO-PHY (theme)

In the new concert hall, the Place des Arts, in Montreal, the quartet completed a solid outing before an enthusiastic crowd, marred only by a rigid adherence to their usual sequence of solos. Ben Riley deserves special commendation for his enchanting use of brushes in both solos and accompaniment. The sequence of titles on the original cover is unfortunately wrong.

Thelonious Monk Quartet Live in Europe 1965
Landscape 903-CD

Charlie Rouse (ts), Monk (p), Larry Gales (b), Ben Riley (d); March 3, 1965:
EVIDENCE / BLUE MONK / FOUR IN ONE / SWEET AND LOVELY / RHYTHM-A-NING / EPISTROPHY / WELL, YOU NEEDN'T / I'M GETTING SENTIMENTAL OVER YOU / TEO / BRIGHT MISSISSIPPI / EPISTROPHY

The concerts begin to sound like one another, but this concert in Olympia is among the best of its type. Especially interesting is 'Bright Mississippi', on which there is some protracted interplay between Monk and Charlie Rouse. The sound is good, although it highlights Monk's distracting foot-stomping.

Sphere
Affinity Aff 20 (RJL 3003)

Charlie Rouse (ts), Monk (p), Larry Gales (b), Ben Riley (d); March

18/20, 1966 (the date on the cover is wrong):
JUST ONE WAY TO SAY I LOVE YOU (p solo) / LULU'S BACK
IN TOWN / JUST A GIGOLO (p solo) / I'M GETTING SEN-
TIMENTAL OVER YOU

Epistrophy
Affinity FA18

*Charlie Rouse (ts), Monk (p), Larry Gales (b), Ben Riley (d); March
18/20, 1966 (the date on the cover is wrong):*
SWEET AND LOVELY / OFF MINOR / CREPUSCULE WITH
NELLIE / EPISTROPHY

A cloud of obscurity envelops these two albums, made in Paris
and broadcast on French radio. Somehow they landed on the Byg
label, which later became Affinity. The recording quality, in any
case, is amazingly good. And they are the only records available
that document Monk's concert routine from this period. Two solo
pieces approximately five minutes in length ('Just One Way' and
'Just a Gigolo') break up the otherwise very extended, often fif-
teen-minute-long quartet performances. All the members of the
band contribute lengthy solos. Larry Gales surprises with his
masterful and earthy bass solos, often 'walking', and Ben Riley
displays his facility with the brushes. Monk and Rouse remain
true to themselves in the best sense. Both albums are collected on
a single CD: *The Paris Concert* (Affinity 74-CD).

Straight, No Chaser
Columbia CS 9451; CD: Columbia 468409

*Charlie Rouse (ts), Monk (p), Larry Gales (b), Ben Riley (d); Novem-
ber 14, 1966:*
I DIDN'T KNOW ABOUT YOU
Same personnel; November 15, 1966:
LOCOMOTIVE
Same personnel; January 10, 1967:

STRAIGHT, NO CHASER / JAPANESE FOLK SONG (KOH-
JOH NO TSUKI) / BETWEEN THE DEVIL AND THE DEEP
BLUE SEA (p solo) / WE SEE

After a lag of some years, CBS finally produced another studio
album by the Monk quartet. All participants seem aware of the
importance of the occasion and play with exceptional focus.

Larry Gales deserves special praise for his masterly bass. The
first piece brings a welcome reunion with 'Locomotive.' Monk's
solo, on which every note counts, is framed by outstanding contributions from Charlie Rouse. Ben Riley had since learned how
to integrate the elegant percussion style he displayed in his solos
with his ensemble style, which was shaped by Monk's rhythmic
ideas. Ellington's 'I Didn't Know' is first presented by the piano
in a trio setting. Rouse, the one-time Ellington saxophonist, then
interprets it as a beautifully lyrical and yet sober ballad.

'Straight, No Chaser' begins with subtle and involved interplay between piano and saxophone. The more Rouse participates,
the less is heard from the piano, until it ceases altogether. Monk
in his solo brims with witty variations on the theme, and demonstrates again his mastery of silence. Gales plays a walking solo
that both makes sense on its own terms, and logically introduces
Ben Riley's eloquent contribution. Before the reprise there is another Rouse encore, structured by the piano.

The 'Japanese Folk Song' has a genuine AABA structure, but the individual sections are only four bars long. It begins in medium-fast tempo. During the rigorously structured saxophone solo a switch is made to double time. Monk's solo is based on the ground-tempo, and makes satisfying play with the mildly exotic harmonies of the theme. Piano and bass then engage in a stirring duet to the accompaniment of the brushes. A saxophone encore leads to the reprise. On his solo performance of 'Between the Devil and the Deep Blue Sea' Monk betrays some difficulties in getting started. He repeatedly interrupts the rhythmic flow, before finally entering into the spirit of the material in stride style. 'We See' again features the quartet in fine form, and brings to an end one of the best albums that CBS produced with Monk.

The Nonet – Live in Paris 1967
France's Concert FCD 113

Charlie Rouse (ts), Monk (p), Larry Gales (b), Ben Riley (d); plus Ray Copeland (tp), Johnny Griffin (ts), Jimmy Cleveland (tb), Phil Woods (as), Clark Terry (tp); November 3, 1967:
RUBY, MY DEAR / WE SEE / EPISTROPHY / OSKA-T / EVIDENCE / BLUE MONK / EPISTROPHY

Nonet is a somewhat misleading title. The concert begins with the quartet, then the quartet plus Ray Copeland, then the quartet plus the remaining horn players except Clark Terry, and finally Clark Terry as soloist plus the octet. The first two numbers are first-class Monk routine. On 'We See' Ray Copeland rises to new heights of eloquence. His somewhat thin trumpet sound on *Monk's Music* had since developed into a powerful blast. The octet, it is true, sounds somewhat clumsy and unrehearsed, but also nicely relaxed. On 'Epistrophy' the Parisian expatriate Johnny Griffin has an inspiring homestand. The second soloist is Copeland. His solo gives the impression of being well planned in advance, though shaky at the start. Monk is next, and shows that here, as throughout the evening, he does not want to come short of the generally high level of play. His approach is exceptionally sly.

'Oska-T' follows the pattern of the December 30, 1963 recording. The soloists are Copeland, Griffin, a rather pallid Jimmy Cleveland, Monk, and Larry Gales. Gales impresses with his double-grip techniques. On 'Evidence' the sequence of solos is: Rouse, Copeland, Phil Woods (who gradually adjusts to the mood of the piece), Monk, and Larry Gales. On 'Evidence', as earlier on 'Oska-T', the horns play occasional riffs, thus proving, as their name implies, that this is a real band, not just a collection of soloists. Clark Terry is a guest star on 'Blue Monk.' His supple, friendly, humorous trumpet style suits the Monk band and the accompaniment of its leader well. Monk actually falls silent after a few of Terry's choruses to just listen and enjoy. The transcription is technically excellent and a real delight. As noted in the biography section (p. 87), it's a shame that CBS did not bring this band into the studio.

Monk Underground
Columbia CS 9632; CD: Columbia 460066

Charlie Rouse (ts), Monk (p), Larry Gales (b), Ben Riley (d); December 14, 1967:

UGLY BEAUTY
Same personnel; December 21, 1967:
BOO BOO'S BIRTHDAY
Same, minus Rouse; February 14, 1968:
EASY STREET / IN WALKED BUD (with Jon Hendricks, vocal) /
RAISE FOUR / THELONIOUS
Same, with Rouse; December 14, 1968:
GREEN CHIMNEYS

Underground Monk is Monk's next-to-last album with CBS, and his last combo record with the label. The music remains good, but the packaging, with the tasteless photo, and the overwrought story presenting 'Captain' Monk as a hero of the subversive movement, shows the direction in which CBS wanted to go with their jazz division. The record suggests that 'underground' protests against the Establishment, and demonstrations against the Vietnam War, were simply 'in' so far as they was concerned. Yet the marketing concept is limited to the cover. Musically, Monk had occasion to present four new compositions. But there seem to have been personal problems within the quartet. Only on 'Ugly Beauty', 'Boo Boo's Birthday', and 'Green Chimneys' does Charlie Rouse participate. 'Thelonious' is expertly covered in trio setting, although the percussion is perhaps a bit too aggressive. 'Ugly Beauty' is a typical Monk ballad in three-four time. As the theme unfolds one gets a feeling of *déjà vu*, or rather *déjà entendu:* Is this 'Ruby, My Dear' or 'Crepuscule with Nellie'? 'Raise Four' is a simple blues riff theme in medium-fast time. Monk's repetition of figures creates and resolves tension over and over.

'Boo Boo's Birthday', a birthday present for his daughter who was visiting the studio, is yet another gloriously odd Monk theme in regular AABA form and medium-fast time. Saxophone and piano work closely together. Monk works the thematic material freely and creatively in his solo. A transitional solo by Rouse leads to the reprise. 'Easy Street' is very conventionally treated in trio format. Monk hardly strays from the theme. 'Green Chimneys' riffs simply in song form, and in the faster tempo the rhythm section finds a fiercely swinging groove. Rouse's playing is lively, and Monk is not sparing of his ironic humor. This piece is also devoted to his beloved daughter and named after the green chimneys of her boarding school. The melody line of 'In Walked Bud' is presented by the bebop singer Jon Hendricks, who also scats a long solo. Monk plays a frugal solo before the reprise. I personally would prefer to hear the piece presented by the trio; yet consider the entire record a worthy summation of Monk's combo career with CBS.

Monk's Blues
Columbia CS 9806; CD: Columbia 475698

Conte Candoli, Freddie Hill, Robert Brookmeyer and Bobby Bryant (tp), Billy Byers and Mike Wimberley (tb), Ernie Watts (as, fl-h), Tom Scott and Gene Cipriano (ts, reeds), Charlie Rouse (ts solos), Ernie Small (bs), Howard Roberts (g), Monk (p), Larry Gales (b), Ben Riley (d), John Guerin (perc), Oliver Nelson (arr, cond); November 19, 1968:
LITTLE ROOTIE TOOTIE / LET'S COOL ONE / STRAIGHT, NO CHASER / REFLECTIONS / MONK'S POINT
Same personnel; November 20, 1968:
JUST A GLANCE AT LOVE / TRINKLE TINKLE / BRIL-

LIANT CORNERS / CONSECUTIVE SECONDS
CD bonus track: 'ROUND MIDNIGHT
With this album CBS' marketing strategy went beyond the packaging (with its rather surrealistic cover) to infect the music itself. The result represents Monk's surrender to the god of commerce and the musical ideal that unites Broadway, Hollywood, and TV. The creator of this sound was Oliver Nelson. He was selected by producer Teo Macero (who once played with Charlie Mingus before producing Miles Davis and Thelonious Monk at CBS) to write big band arrangements for Monk compositions in a grand, all-American manner. To give the production some popular appeal, Macero extended the commission to include two of his own compositions, one of which was certainly pinched from an old musical.

Monk participates on this venture as the solo star and effaces his personal style as much as he can—perhaps out of embarrassment. The bombastic sound of the big orchestra buries all trace of Monk's musical personality under layers of ooze, and absolutely murders Monk's compositions. Even a hit album should not succeed at the cost of betraying its musical soul. For Monk the consequence of this betrayal was clear: with this album his association with CBS came to an end.

Monk's Blues is the second disc of the CBS double album *Who's Afraid of the Big Band Monk* (CS 32892).

Always Know
Columbia JG 35720; CD: 469185-2

Columbia recordings that were passed over for release at the time of recording were later issued on this 1979 double album. Because they agree in spirit with their respective sessions, in what follows we will list only the name of the cut, and give references to the corresponding album and recording session. The one exception is the piano solo 'This Is My Story, This Is My Song', which is actually the hymn 'Blessed Assurance'–an allusion by the mature Monk to his youthful *Wanderjahre.* All cuts on *Always Know* are unedited.

Titles in the sequence on the double CD: THIS IS MY STORY, THIS IS MY SONG (*Straight, No Chaser,* November 14, 1966) / CRISS CROSS (*Miles & Monk At Newport,* July 4, 1963) / LIGHT BLUE (*Big Band And Quartet In Concert,* December 30, 1963) / MONK'S DREAM (*Monk's Dream,* November 2, 1962) / PLAYED TWICE (here unedited; *Big Band And Quartet In Concert,* December 30, 1963) / DARN THAT DREAM (*Solo Monk,* March 2, 1965) / EPISTROPHY (*It's Monk's Time,* January 30, 1964) / COMING ON THE HUDSON (*Criss Cross,* November 6, 1962)/ BYE-YA / INTROSPECTION (*Solo Monk,* March 2, 1965) / EASY STREET (here unedited; *Underground,* February 14, 1968) / SHUFFLE BOIL (alternate take; *It's Monk's Time,* March 9, 1964) / HONEYSUCKLE ROSE (*Live At The Jazz Workshop,* November 3, 1964)

Final recordings

Monk in Tokyo
Far East 60006-LP

Paul Jeffrey (ts), Monk (p), Larry Ridley (b), Lenny McBrowne (d); October 4, 1970
STRAIGHT, NO CHASER / DON'T BLAME ME / EVIDENCE
Same personnel and same date, but also with Toshiyuki Miyama and The New Herd
'ROUND MIDNIGHT / BLUE MONK

The Man I Love
Black Lion BL-197

Monk (p solo); November 15, 1971:
TRINKLE TINKLE (take 2) / LITTLE ROOTIE TOOTIE / THE MAN I LOVE

Monk (p), Al McKibbon (b), Art Blakey (d); November 15, 1971:
MISTERIOSO / RUBY, MY DEAR / CREPUSCULE WITH
NELLIE (take 4)

Nice Work in London
Freedom PA-9731

Monk (p solo); November 15, 1971:
TRINKLE TINKLE (take 3) / SOMETHING IN BLUE / DARN
THAT DREAM / NICE WORK IF YOU CAN GET IT / BLUE
SPHERE / CREPUSCULE WITH NELLIE (take 2)

Blue Sphere
Black Lion BLM 51051

Monk (p solo); November 15, 1971:
SOMETHING IN BLUE / JACKIE-ING / LITTLE ROOTIE
TOOTIE / MY MELANCHOLY BABY

Something in Blue
Black Lion BL-152

Monk (p solo); November 15, 1971:
SOMETHING IN BLUE / JACKIE-ING / NICE WORK IF
YOU CAN GET IT / BLUE SPHERE
Monk (p), Al McKibbon (b), Art Blakey (d); November 15, 1971:
EVIDENCE (take 2) / HACKENSACK (take 2) / NUTTY (take 2)/
CRISS CROSS

The material from the preceding three albums is collected on the
following CDs:

The London Collection: Volume 1
Black Lion BLCD 760101

Monk (p solo); November 15, 1971:
TRINKLE TINKLE (take 3) / CREPUSCULE WITH NELLIE
(take 2) / DARN THAT DREAM / LITTLE ROOTIE TOOTIE /
MEET ME TONIGHT IN DREAMLAND / NICE WORK IF

YOU CAN GET IT / MY MELANCHOLY BABY / JACKIE-ING / LOVER MAN / BLUE SPHERE

The London Collection: Volume 2
Black Lion BLCD 7601161

Monk (p), Al McKibbon (b), Art Blakey (d); November 15, 1971:
EVIDENCE (take 2) / MISTERIOSO / CREPUSCULE WITH NELLIE (take 4) / I MEAN YOU / CRISS CROSS/ RUBY, MY DEAR / NUTTY (take 2) / HACKENSACK (take 2)

The London Collection: Volume 3
Black Lion BLCD 760142

Monk (p solo); November 15, 1971:
TRINKLE TINKLE (take 2) / THE MAN I LOVE / SOMETHING IN BLUE / INTROSPECTION (take 1) / TRINKLE TINKLE (take 1) / CHORDIALLY
Monk (p), Al McKibbon (b), Art Blakey (d); November 15, 1971:
CREPUSCULE WITH NELLIE (take 3) / NUTTY (take 1) INTROSPECTION (take 2) / HACKENSACK (take 1) / EVI-DENCE (take 1)

The release in two different countries of four discs recorded in London explains the overlap of numbers. Historians of jazz have reason to be grateful to producer Alan Bates that the discography of Thelonious Monk's studio recordings does not end with the travesty *Monk's Blues.*

The series of live recordings had already come to an end the previous year with the release of the concert that the Monk quartet gave in Tokyo on April 10, 1970. On this occasion Monk played with tenor saxophonist Paul Jeffrey, bassist Larry Ridley, and drummer Lenny McBrowne. They play Monk classics, and the aesthetic approach of the band is based on the quartet with Charlie Rouse. To be sure, Paul Jeffrey and Lenny McBrowne were not as deeply imbued with Monk's world of sound as their predecessors in the classic quartet, and they cannot compensate with a distinctive individuality. Still, they perform capably enough, and Monk is stoically true to himself. On "Round Midnight' and 'Blue Monk' the quartet is unobtrusively accompanied by Toshiyuki Miyama's New Herd orchestra.

The first world tour of The Giants of Jazz all-star troupe ended on November 14, 1971 with a concert in London. Alan Bates took the initiative in enlisting Monk the following day for an extended recording session with his Black Lion label. Monk spent six hours in the studio. The first three were devoted to solo performances. He was then joined by Art Blakey and Al McKibbon. The solo recordings distinguish themselves by an especially relaxed air. Two blues, 'Something in Blue' and 'Blue Sphere', were pure improvisations, and are the highlights. It is true that Monk earlier in his life may have had greater fluency at his command, but now he is aware of his technical limitations, does not overreach, and sounds as if he were playing for himself. He sticks to slow or medium-fast tempos, with deep respect for the masters of the Harlem stride tradition. Over a left hand that jumps, and occasionally sketches contrasting lines, Monk's right hand supplies conventional figures, always making repeated drafts, however, on his peculiar harmonic world. For the listener who is devoted to the original performances of the remaining numbers, these new readings are not as persuasive. But that may just be because the inner ear associates the themes with their first performance. In any case, the exploration of the themes in the solos is always engaging.

The trio recordings, anchored by Blakey's propulsive beat, have something of the powerfully swinging angularity of the earlier Monk. Al McKibbon's bass, unfortunately, is not properly recorded; it sounds as if it is keyed to a faulty microphone. His lines, insofar as they can be heard, also sound like they are missing the harmonic boat. Monk is said to have been mad at him during the session since he was no longer familiar with these early compositions although they had recorded some of them together for Blue Note. Perhaps that is why he chose to play 'Crepuscule with Nellie' alone at first, to familiarize Al McKibbon with the number, even though the trio session was underway.

The London recordings make one thing clear: in congenial surroundings Monk was still ready to apply himself and make an effort. This leads to a sad reflection. What might have happened had CBS taken the same care to produce him that they did Miles Davis? Monk was ready to try the Hollywood adventure with Oliver Nelson. Probably he would have agreed to a more artistically satisfying adventure that teamed him with challenging individuals such as the bassist Ron Carter, drummer Ed Blackwell, or tenor saxophonist Joe Henderson, in a carefully conceived production. His life history suggests that Monk was a phlegmatic personality, who needed to be prodded from without.

One has cause to regret another missed opportunity in connection with the London recordings. The Giants of Jazz made a stop in Paris. Monk might have teamed up with Kenny Clarke, the venerated expatriate, and the reigning European master of the swing 'walking bass', Pierre Michelot. That would have added a dimension to Monk's trio recordings not heard before.

The Giants of Jazz in Berlin '71
EmArcy CD-834567

Dizzy Gillespie (tp), Sonny Stitt (as, ts), Kai Winding (tb), Monk (p), Al McKibbon (b), Art Blakey (d); November 5, 1971:
INTRODUCTION / BLUE 'N' BOOGIE / 'ROUND MIDNIGHT / TOUR DE FORCE / LOVER MAN / TIN TIN DEO / EVERYTHING HAPPENS TO ME / A NIGHT IN TUNISIA

The Giants of Jazz
Concord Jazz, The George Wein Collection GW-3004; CD: CCD 43004
Dizzy Gillespie (tp), Monk (p), Kai Winding (tb), Sonny Stitt (as, ts),

Al McKibbon (b), Art Blakey (d); November 12, 1971 (the date on the cover is wrong):
STRAIGHT, NO CHASER / THELONIOUS / SWEET AND LOVELY / DON'T BLAME ME / I'LL WAIT FOR YOU / EPISTROPHY

The Giants of Jazz
Recorded Live at the Victoria Theater in London
Atlantic SD 2-905

Dizzy Gillespie (tp, p), Monk (p), Kai Winding (tb), Sonny Stitt (as, ts), Al McKibbon (b), Art Blakey (d); November 14, 1971:
TIN TIN DEO / ALLEN'S ALLEY / WOODY 'N' YOU / NIGHT IN TUNISIA / BLUE 'N' BOOGIE / 'ROUND MIDNIGHT / TOUR DE FORCE / EVERYTHING HAPPENS TO ME / BLUE MONK

The Giants of Jazz recordings will be reviewed collectively here for the sake of thematic continuity, though some are actually earlier than the Black Lion recordings discussed above. Monk's last legitimately recorded performances took place in this setting.

Prior to their appearance in London, which was the occasion for the legendary Black Lion recordings, the Giants of Jazz appeared at the Berlin Jazz Festival. The performance was quite similar to the London show. An interesting contribution by Monk comes on 'Lover Man', where he spaces out a series of minimal motifs. As with all the appearances he made with the The Giants of Jazz, Monk truly surprises with the accommodating style of his accompaniment. And so with Monk's first and last official release a circle is closed, because he was also a deferential accompanist on his first record date, with Coleman Hawkins–Monk, normally the terror of horn players, once execrated by Miles Davis on this account.

Compared with the rough sound of the Atlantic sides (discussed next), the Concord album is better balanced and more pleasing to the ear. Yet the playing itself is lacking in polish and vigor, and no jam-session revelry emerges to breathe life into the workmanlike proceedings. Monk is represented by three compositions, a higher proportion than usual in the Giants repertoire. Unfortunately it is made more than ever clear in these studio recordings how little of Monk's own personality survived in this setting. The Giants treat 'Straight, No Chaser' as simply a blowing vehicle for a blues jam session. On 'Thelonious', it is true, Monk gets a chance to lead. The horns contribute very simple head arrangements, which, though played with precision, are far removed from the spirit of the original performance, or from the performances with the Hall Overton orchestra. 'Epistrophy' is subject to an interesting treatment: a persistent rhythmic riff transforms it into an effective funk number. On the other pieces, Monk, who had long distanced himself from bebop, is reduced in this rigid bebop context to the role of subordinate accompanist. Even in this reduced role his musical personality is discernible.

On November 14, 1971, the Giants of Jazz did two shows in London's Victoria Theater. George Wein produced a double album for Atlantic from the tapes. The music is of the robust jam-session variety, similar to the 'Jazz at the Philharmonic' concerts that Norman Granz produced in the fifties. The complex arrangements made possible by a sextet are for the most part passed over in favor of flashy riffs, and the ensemble passages are uneven. The sound suffers considerably from the fact that Al McKibbon is not on good terms with his amp or microphone; the bass sounds like it is emanating from a plastic box. As a vibrant live session, this double album certainly has something to offer. Where else, at this time, can one hear Sonny Stitt with such a cooking rhythm section? But the music is stereotypical bebop throughout. One cannot really speak of Monk's distinctive sound in the performance of "Round Midnight.' If one musician shaped these recordings, it is Dizzy Gillespie. He is responsible, in fact, for most of the compositions.

The record opens with 'Tin Tin Deo.' It is delivered as a trumpet–bass duo, during which McKibbon sounds a little out of sorts. During the bass solo Gillespie plays a simple and affecting piano accompaniment. Monk first touches the keys during the piece's final bars, when the ensemble comes in. Dizzy Gillespie's 'Night in Tunisia' features Art Blakey. A brief trumpet solo precedes the drum's turn. Gillespie's 'Woody 'n' You' follows in moderately fast time. After effective solos by alto, trombone, and trumpet, there is a piano solo. We have already mentioned Monk's polite accompaniment. His solo is distinguished by single-note runs over two choruses. Only his left hand really 'monks.' In the third chorus the single note lines congeal to form chord clusters. These clusters are pushed and pulled through the changes as daring off-beat accents.

The next piece, 'Tour De Force', is again by Gillespie, and is exactly as advertised: a solo parade in fast mid-tempo, featuring trumpet, tenor, and piano. The playing of the piano is similar to that on 'Woody 'n' You.' Excitement builds when the muted trumpet, accompanied by the bass, plays a duet with the drums. A competent bass solo relieves the tension before the reprise. Denzil Best's 'Allen's Alley' is another horn parade with drum solo, taken up-tempo. Monk's Bud Powell-style accompaniment is again notable. The next number, 'Blue 'n' Boogie', is another one of Gillespie's. After the theme there is a piano solo that steeps dissonant single notes in the blues, and 'monks' with the left hand in imitation of the theme. A parade of solos follows, consisting of horns and drums. Before each one the Dizzy Gillespie riff that was made famous by Miles Davis is played.

'Everything Happens to Me' is purely a showcase for Sonny Stitt's alto saxophone. With 'Blue Monk' there is finally a Monk composition. Following the four-bar piano introduction the theme emerges rich and beautiful in the ensemble. But by the time of the alto solo Art Blakey has reverted with such infectious enthusiasm

to that shuffling back-beat for which he was famous, that the entire piece is transformed into a piece of Jazz Messengers music.
That applies not only to the horns. Monk himself takes Blakey's
bait, and plays a succulent solo based on the theme and rooted in
the blues, with a nod in the direction of Bobby Timmons. After
the bass solo and before the reprise there is a dense whirl from
the drums that is slightly fluffed.

The record ends with "Round Midnight.' Now the arrangement possibilities inherent in a sextet are finally exploited. Dizzy
Gillespie must have had a tight rein on this number. After the
famous *tutti* introduction that he wrote he plays a cadence, whereupon Monk develops the A-section of the theme in a rather conventional manner. Sonny Stitt on the alto plays a charming B-
section. The horn accompaniment in the A-sections recalls the
Blue Note performance, and the pointed interpolations in the B-
section hark back to the classic Miles Davis recording. The con-
cluding A-section is voiced with feeling by Kai Winding. A Monk
chorus follows, over Art Blakey's double-time. It represents just
about the quintessence of the exploration of this material. The
next A-sections are delivered on muted trumpet, accompanied
only by bass and piano. On the B-section the drums come in. The
A-section is again reserved to Monk. The number ends with four
bars of the famous Gillespie epilogue from the ensemble, and a
trumpet coda.

At least a new generation of listeners was able to experience
Monk live with The Giants of Jazz. Thanks are due to the businessman and impresario George Wein, that he thought of Monk
in connection with this project. In 1971 things were not going so
well for Monk, and the world tour of the Giants, on which Nellie
was able to accompany him, instilled in him a positive new outlook, at least for a time.

Straight, No Chaser
Columbia SC 45358; CD: Columbia 453582

STRAIGHT, NO CHASER / PANNONICA / TRINKLE
TINKLE / UGLY BEAUTY (rehearsal) / UGLY BEAUTY / EVI-
DENCE / I MEAN YOU (rehearsal and performance) / LULU'S
BACK IN TOWN / DON'T BLAME ME / SWEETHEART OF
ALL MY DREAMS / 'ROUND MIDNIGHT
CD bonus track: EPISTROPHY

This record is a special case. It is an audio adaptation by Orrin
Keepnews of Charlotte Zwerin's film *Straight, No Chaser*. The first
title derives from the Columbia album of the same name. There
is a voice-over describing Monk's life. The second number is quite
moving. Monk recorded it especially for Baroness Pannonica de
Koenigswarter, probably in September 1956, but certainly before
the *Brilliant Corners* recording. It represents, therefore, the debut
recording of the piece. It includes a loving spoken tribute by the
composer himself, usually a man of few words. 'Lulu's Back in
Town' comes from the same private collection. It is playfully af-
fectionate. 'Trinkle Tinkle' comes from the Jazzland album, and
the full version of 'Ugly Beauty' is on *Underground*. 'Evidence',
'Epistrophy', and 'I Mean You' are recordings of the octet's guest
appearance in Sweden in October/November 1967. The rehearsal

demonstrates how ill prepared the band was for the gig. The solos by Ray Copeland (tp), Phil Woods (as), Charlie Rouse (ts), Johnny Griffin (ts), and even Monk himself, are wooden. Larry Gales and Ben Riley were on bass and drums. Through "Round Midnight", however, (of which only the last chorus is reproduced here), the other numbers are stride piano versions of popular songs, and great fun. 'Don't Blame Me' was recorded in the autumn of 1957 in Atlanta. 'Sweetheart', as well as "Round Midnight", were recorded near the beginning of 1968 on a wretched piano at the Village Vanguard.

Films and Videos

The following is a selection of the most notable films and videos. Most of this material is available from The Jazz Store, P.O. Box 917, Upper Montclair NJ 07043-0917, Tel. (800) 558-9513.

The Sound of Jazz

December 8, 1957. 58 mins. (b & w). Prod. Robert Herridge, Dir. Jack Smight. Kay Productions KJ 13 (VHS Green Line 2). A CBS television broadcast featuring Monk, Billy Holiday, Coleman Hawkins and many other jazz musicians. Monk (p), Ahmed Abdul-Malik (b), and Osie Johnson (d) play 'Blue Monk.' See chapter one above for a description of this event.

Jazz on a Summer's Day

July 8, 1958, Newport. 85 mins. (color). Dir. Burt Stern. LaserDisc CSVF-1394 or New Yorker Video. Monk (p), Henry Grimes (b), and Roy Haynes (d) play 'Blue Monk', while camera mainly shows sailboats off Newport. Other performers include Gerry Mulligan, Anito O'Day, Chico Hamilton, *et al.*

Jazz 625 – Giants of Jazz Golden Era
Thelonious Monk. Volume One

Marquee Club, London, March 14, 1965. 34 mins. (b & w). PNV 1035 (video and laserdisc). The quartet with Rouse, Gales, and Riley perform 'Epistrophy', 'Criss Cross', and 'Well, You Needn't.'

Jazz 625 – Giants of Jazz Golden Era
Thelonious Monk. Volume Two

Same location, date, and personnel. 35 mins. (b & w). PNV 1036 (video and laserdisc). Quartet performs 'Straight, No Chaser', 'Hackensack', 'Rhythm-a-ning', and 'Epistrophy.'

Monk in Europe

46 mins. (b & w and color). VIDJAZZ 18 (video). The quartet with Rouse, Gales, and Riley (London 1965) perform 'Straight, No Chaser', 'Hackensack', 'Rhythm-a-ning', and 'Epistrophy.' Monk solo (Berlin 1969) performs 'Sophisticated Lady', 'Caravan', and 'Solitude.'

Music in Monk's Time

1983. 60 mins. (color and b & w). Prod. Stephen Rice, Paul C. Matthews, and John Goodhue. Sonfilm International Production. LaserDisc CBS Sony CSLM-793. Jon Hendricks narrates Monk's life, illustrated by extended clips from performances by the quartet featuring Rouse, Gales, and Riley. Hendricks also sings with an all-star group playing Monk compositions. Thelonious Jr. reminisces about his father.

Straight, No Chaser

1989. 89 mins. (color and b & w). Prod. Charlotte Zwerin and Bruce Ricker. Exec. Prod. Clint Eastwood. Dir. Charlotte Zwerin. Warner Bros. Home Video or LaserDisc CBS WV-11896. Most complete documentary of the man and his music; shots from a recording session, interviews with his personal manager as well as his road manager in 1967, with Nica de Koenigswarter, T.S. Monk Jr., and fellow musicians; private shots from the Monks abroad; extensive footage of the 1967 tour complemented by excerpts from historic film documents.

American Composer
1991. 60 mins. (color and b & w). Prod. Toby Byron, Richard Saylor. Dir. Matthew Seig. EAST STINSON Inc. Masters of Jazz Series. LaserDisc NTSC VAVJ-217. Also available as video, or NTV (PAL) 0017. Randy Weston, Barry Harris, Billy Taylor, Ben Riley, Orrin Keepnews, Thelonious Monk Jr., and Marion White (Monk's sister) remember Monk. Also includes excellent material from footage of classic quartet performances.

A Great Day in Harlem
1995. 60 mins. (color and b &w). Dir. Jean Bach. Wienerworld Presentations Video *(TJS)*. The history behind Art Kane's famous Jazz Portrait Harlem 1958. Zooming in and out of the picture, the film interweaves archival footage and rare interviews. Dizzy Gillespie, Art Blakey and Johnny Griffin remember Monk.

du, Thelonious Monk CD-ROM
Zurich 1997. Word & Vision, prod. (No distributor at press time.) Likely to be the first interactive jazz CD-ROM. You enter an imaginary jazz club with Monk playing there. On the wall there are posters on which you can click for all kinds of information about Monk's life, music, recordings, and related themes such as 'Monk and the jazz community', 'New York as the jazz capital of the world', and 'the socio-economic background to Monk's time.' There is also a glossary of specifically African-American terms.

Appendix A:
A Representative Monk Collection

The preceding discography has been designed as a faithful and detailed guide to Monk's recorded work. The discussion there should help buyers make informed choices from the Monk legacy. But the sheer number of recordings may be overwhelming, and the newcomer to his music might welcome some advice as to where to begin. Monkologists debate whether the early Blue Note and Prestige recordings reflect Monk's uniqueness better than the elaborate and varied Riverside productions, or whether in fact the Columbia quartet albums are the ultimate expression of his art. Personally I have come to love all but a few (including the bootlegs).

The obvious starting point is the Blue Note recordings. Yet these may be less appealing to a neophyte who may not at first recognize what sets them apart from other historic bebop recordings. Since Monk was a unique, uncompromising figure who was true to himself from the beginning to the end of his recorded history, the chronological element is less important for our choice than it would be for other musicians. So I do not hesitate to nominate *Always Know* (Columbia 469185-2; all references to CD editions except where noted) as the album to begin with. It is a sampler representing Monk in different settings. Even though it may not contain the very best material from the individual sessions, it represents the whole scope of Monk's music at the peak of his career. He performs solo, as well as with his quartet and his legendary big band. Most of the tracks are of superb sound quality.

As the next step I would recommend *Solo 1954* (Vogue 111502). After years of frustration Monk finally got the chance to express himself freely, all alone. Determined to make his mark he launches into daringly probing interpretations of eight originals and one standard. The edgy quality of this music can still be felt today; and this feeling is probably close to the reactions listeners had on first hearing Monk's Blue Note records.

The Vogue CD, however, might be hard to find. As an alternative I suggest *The London Collection: Volume 1* (Black Lion BLCD 760101). This might seem paradoxical at first; but this document from Monk's last recording session under his own name has a similar character. It is as if Monk knew that this was his last chance to express himself, and so the element of risk-taking is again prominent.

Now the listener will be ready for the Blue Note recordings. The price for the four-CD boxed set of *The Complete Blue Note Recordings* (CDP 830363) is quite reasonable at most dealers, so why not buy the whole thing? If it is too costly, however, or if the sound quality is felt to be too 'archaeological', one of the two *Genius of Modern Music* CDs (Blue Note 781510/511) should do as well.

For listeners who like contrasts the next step could be the legendary Miles Davis all-star recording session from December 24, 1954, either on *Miles Davis and the Modern Jazz Giants* (Prestige LP 7150–complete session) or on the Miles Davis CD *Bags' Groove* (OJC 245). I am certainly not alone in regarding the first take of 'Bags' Groove' as one of the most beautiful jazz recordings ever made. And it proves my point that at this time Monk could be perceived as someone playing Cool Jazz, and yet as a 'funky' pianist too.

Having approached Monk's Riverside period from both chronological sides it is time to dive in. For me the definitive Riverside record is *Brilliant Corners* (OJC 026). It contains three strikingly new compositions which count among his most innovative. Tenor giant and Monk disciple Sonny Rollins is heard to good advantage, and Monk himself is brilliant. Another must from the Riverside years is *Thelonious Monk with John Coltrane* (OJC 039). For those not afraid of historic-sounding records *Live at the Five Spot: Discovery!* (Blue Note CDP 799786), recorded by Coltrane's wife with amateur portable equipment, is also indispensable. Made after Coltrane was no longer a regular member of the quartet but just sitting in, it still manages to convey the rapport these two geniuses of modern music had developed during their months together at the club.

Now it is time to consider Monk's trio recordings. I recommend *The Unique Thelonious Monk* (OJC 064). It is a good example of Monk's treatment of other composers' material.

By now the listener will have developed an ear for Monk's music and a sense of what he or she prefers. Still, as a final piece of advice I return to our starting point and suggest that they acquire the discs containing the sessions from which their favorite tracks on *Always Know* derive. For quartet performances I personally consider *Monk's Dream* (Columbia 40786) essential; and for Monk in a big-band context, *Monk Big Band and Quartet in Concert* (Columbia 476898).

Two more favorites of mine not yet mentioned are *Art Blakey's Jazz Messengers with Thelonious Monk* (Atlantic 781332-2), and *Five by Monk by Five* (OJC 362).

Appendix B:
A Musical Glossary

Throughout this book, a number of musical expressions are used that the lay reader may not be familiar with. With this reader in mind, a glossary of the more frequent terms is appended here.

Rhythm

The key term here is **beat**. This is the basic pulse underlying measured music and the unit by which musical time is calculated.

The grouping of beats in a regular pattern (the **bar** or **measure**) defined by accentuation is called **meter**. Meter is expressed in terms of the number of beats of a certain value that occur in the bar, often expressed as the **time signature**. An example would be 4/4, the most common time signature in jazz, and the time signature of nearly all Monk's tunes. It means that there are four beats to the bar, and that each has the value of a quarter note.

The grouping of beats into the metrical unit of the bar creates relatively stronger and weaker positions. In 4/4 time, the first beat of the bar is the strongest, the third beat is the next strongest, and the second and the fourth are weakest. Usually the first beat, 'the one', is referred to as the **downbeat**. The terms for any beat other than the downbeat are **offbeat** or **afterbeat**. 'Afterbeat' is essentially a neutral term, whereas 'offbeat' is often used in contexts where the expected accentuation is subverted, and especially where the downbeat is replaced by a rest, or carried over from the preceding bar.

In 4/4 time the weakest beats, the two and the four, are also called **backbeats**. In certain forms of jazz these beats are consistently stressed, and in modern jazz the drummer usually plays the high-hat or sock cymbal on them. The bassist, on the other hand, executes four even quarter notes, playing **four to the bar**.

When in a certain meter or time signature the accents are grouped in a pattern different from that of the basic meter, there is **meter within meter**. In Monk's music this often occurs as a grouping of units of three quarter notes over the basic pulse of four beats to the bar. This specific from of 'meter within meter' is called **three against four**.

When a note is not divided normally intó two notes of the next smaller value (e.g. a half note into two quarter notes), but into three, these three are a **triplet**. A **quadruplet**, in turn, is a group of four notes of equal time value made to be played in the time of three; and a **quintuplet** is a group of five notes of equal value to be played in the time of four.

Rubato is a feature of performance whereby the performer takes liberties with the prescribed tempo of a piece, delaying the beat within a phrase, and then (in recompense) often accelerating it in a subsequent phrase.

Harmonic and Melodic Form

In jazz, as in music generally, tonality is defined by scales, fixed patterns of alternating whole steps (whole tones), and half steps (semitones). Longer runs consisting of semitones only, which are called **chromatic runs**, or of whole tones only, called **whole tone runs**, overrun tonality or blur it.

The harmonic structure of a piece of music is often referred to as its **vertical** structure, whereas its melodic structure is the **horizontal** one.

In traditional jazz and bebop, a tune is associated with a fixed harmonic pattern, the **changes** or **chord changes**, also called

form by musicians. It is over this form that musicians improvise.

The two most common forms are **the blues**, a harmonic movement normally consisting of twelve bars, and employing the blues scale with the associated **blue notes**; and the **song form**, usually consisting of thirty-two bars, subdivided into an **A-section**—a pattern of eight bars with a distinct melody, which is repeated—and a contrasting harmonic and melodic pattern of eight bars, the **B-section**, also called the **bridge**, **release**, or **inside**. This is followed, in turn, by a recapitulation of the A-section. The whole thus constitutes an **AABA** form. When a section is repeated in a slightly altered form, then it is marked **A′**, **B′**, etc. One run through the whole form or pattern of changes is called a **chorus**. Often a solo consists of one or more complete choruses.

In jazz, the playing of the melody is mainly associated with wind instruments or, in jazz argot, 'horns.' Since they usually produce only one note at a time, they necessarily create **single note lines** or simply **blowing lines**. So when such lines are produced on keyboard instruments, which are usually made to play more than one note at a time, this style of playing is characterized in these terms.

Sometimes a section of the ensemble repeats a melodic pattern or motif several times in order to enhance the emotion created by the soloist; played thus, the motif becomes a **riff**.

A tune or song that can be expected to be recognized by its chord structure, and possibly by an arrangement shared among professional musicians, is called a **standard**.

Descant refers to the treble, or upper register, of a number.

Legato refers to a style of playing in which notes are played in a smooth and continuous flow, as opposed to being broken up in **staccato** fashion.

An **arpeggio** is a series of notes played in (usually rapid) succession, as opposed to simultaneously in a chord.

Sources

Anonymous. 'Loneliest Monk; Jazzman Thelonious Monk.' *Time* February 28, 1964.

Bächli, Dieter (ed.). 'Misterioso. Jazzlegende Thelonious Monk.' *du* March 1994.

Berendt, Joachim Ernst. *Das Jazzbuch: von Rag bis Rock.* Frankfurt am Main 1973.

Blumenthal, Bob. Liner notes for *Thelonious Monk: The Complete Blue Note Recordings.* Blue Note CDP 830363.

Bijl, Leen, and Fred Canté. *Monk on Records.* 2nd edition, Amsterdam 1985.

Buhles, Günter. 'Thelonious Monk, Jazz Composer.' *Jazz Podium* March and April 1978.

Buin, Yves. *Thelonious Monk.* Paris 1988.

Carr, Ian. *Miles Davis. A Critical Biography.* London 1982.

Chesnel, Jacques. *et al.*, 'Qui était donc Thelonious Monk?' *Jazz Hot* March 1982.

Cuscuna, Michael. Liner notes for *The Complete Blue Note Recordings of Thelonious Monk.* Mosaic MR 4-101.

____. Liner notes for *The Complete Black Lion and Vogue Recordings of Thelonious Monk.* Mosaic MR 4-112.

Davis, Miles, with Quincy Troupe. *Miles, The Autobiography.* New York 1989.

Doerschuk, Bob, Ran Blake, *et al.* 'Thelonious Monk 1917-1982.' *Keyboard* July 1982.

Duthil, Alex, and Michel Lequime. 'Thelonious Monk, ou comment bougent les pierres.' *Jazz Hot* June 1974.

Feather, Leonard. *The Encyclopedia of Jazz.* London 1961.

____. 'Blindfold Test; Cal Tjader.' *Down Beat* June 17, 1965.

____. 'Blindfold Test; Thelonious Monk.' *Down Beat* April 21, 1966.

Fitterling, Thomas. Interviews with Mal Waldron, 1987, 1996, 1996. Unpublished.

____. 'Mal Waldron–Der Mann der zweimal lebte.' *Rondo* April 1995.

____. 'Mal Waldron wird 70.' *Jazz Podium* September 1995.

____. 'Historical and Socio-economic Background to the Life and Works of Thelonious Monk'; 'Jazz Capital New York City'; 'Thelonious Monk and the Jazz Community.' *Word & Vision: Thelonious Monk CD-ROM Windows,* Zurich 1997.

Gillespie, Dizzy, and Al Fraser. *Dizzy, To Be Or Not To Bop.* London 1980.

Gimbre, Jean-Louis. 'Kenny Clarke; de Pittsburgh à Montreuil.' *Jazz Magazine* March 1985.

Gitler, Ira. 'Ira Gitler interviews Thelonious Monk.' *Metronome* March 1957.

____. *Jazzmasters of the Forties.* New York 1966.

____. *Swing to Bop.* Oxford and New York 1985.

Goldberg, J. *Jazzmasters of the Fifties.* 2nd edition, London and New York 1980.

Gonzales, Pearl. 'Monk Talk.' *Down Beat* October 28, 1971.

Hawes, Hampton, Don Asher. *Raise Up Off Me.* New York 1979.

Hennessey, *The Story of Kenny Clarke.* London and New York 1990.

Hentoff, Nat. 'The Private World of Thelonious Monk.'

Esquire April 1960.

_____. *The Jazz Life.* New York 1961.

_____. *Jazz Is.* New York 1984.

Hodeir, André. *Les Mondes du Jazz.* Paris 1970.

_____. *Jazz: Its Evolution and Essence.* 2nd edition, New York 1975.

Jepsen, Jorgen Grunnet. *A Discography of Thelonious Monk and Bud Powell.* Copenhagen 1969.

Jones, Leroi. *Black Music.* New York 1967.

Jost, Ekkehard. *Sozialgeschichte des Jazz in den USA.* Frankfurt am Main 1986.

Keepnews, Orrin. *The View from Within.* Oxford and New York 1988.

Kernfeld, Barry (ed.), *The New Grove Dictionary of Jazz.* London and New York 1988.

Kotlowitz, Robert. 'Monk Talk.' *Harper's* September 1961.

Lindenmaier, H. Lukas. 'Thelonious Monk Diskographie.' *Jazz Podium* April and May 1982.

Mansfield, Howard. Thelonious Monk home page: http://www.achilles.net/~howardm/tsmonk.html.

Paudras, Francis. *La danse des Infidèles.* Paris 1986.

Peck, Ira. 'The Piano Man Who Dug Be-Bop.' *P.M.'s Sunday Picture News* (Magazine Section) February 22, 1948.

Piacentino, Giuseppe. 'Monk, Il Cammino sull' Abisso.' *Musica Jazz* April 1982.

Polillo, Arrigo. *Jazz. Geschichte und Persönlichkeiten der afroamerikanischen Musik.* Munich and Berlin 1978.

Ponzio, Jacques, and François Postif. *Blue Monk, un Portrait de Thelonious.* Arles 1995.

Priestley, Brian, and Dave Gelly. *Thelonious Monk.* In the series *The Jazz Masters* London 1977.

Réda, Jacques. 'D'où vient le prophète.' *Jazz Magazine* June 1979.

Réda, Jacques, *et al.* 'Spécial Monk.' *Jazz Magazine* April 1982.

Renaud, Henri. 'Bebop Highlights.' *Jazz Hot* May 1974.

Ruedi, Peter. 'Just Play These Goddam Drums!' *du*, December 1996.

Russell, Ross. *Bird Lives.* London 1973.

Shapiro, Nat, and Nat Hentoff. *Hear Me Talkin' to Ya.* New York 1955.

Scheffner, Manfred. *Bielefelder Katalog; Jazz* Stuttgart 1996.

Sheridan, Chris. 'Porträt eines Einsiedlers, Thelonious Monk.' *Jazz Podium* April 1982.

Simon, G. *Simon Says: The Sights and Sounds of the Swing Era.* New York 1971.

Spellman, A.B. *Four Lives in the Bebop Business.* 2nd edition, New York 1985.

Thelonious Monk Institute of Jazz, Private correspondence with the author, confirming dates of birth and death of Barbara Monk and Barbara 'Boo Boo' Monk.

Werther, Iron. *Bebop.* Frankfurt 1988.

de Wilde, Laurent. *Monk.* Paris 1996.

Williams, Martin (ed.). *The Art of Jazz* 2nd edition, New York 1960.

Williams, Martin. *The Jazz Tradition.* 2nd edition, New York 1983.

_____. *Jazz Heritage.* Oxford and New York 1985.

Wilmer, Valerie. 'Monk on Monk,' *Down Beat,* June 3, 1965.

_____. *Jazz People,* London 1970.

Wilson, John, S. 'Thelonious Monk, Unworldly from Way Back.' *The New York Times* December 29, 1963.

Wilson, Peter Niklas. 'Versuch über das Monkische.' *Jazzresearch (19),* Graz 1987.

Wittner, Gary, and Ira Braus. 'T.S. Monk on T.S. Monk.' *Coda* May 1993.

Index of Album and CD Titles